A *is for* Adam
The Gospel from Genesis

Ken and Mally Ham

Illustrated by
Dan Lietha

Master
Books

A is for Adam
The Gospel from Genesis

First printing: 1995
Eighth printing: March 2001

ISBN: 0-89051-207-8

Color and black and white illustrations by Dan Lietha
Illustration concepts by Ken Ham and Dan Lietha

Dan Lietha lives in Kentucky and is an illustrator for Answers in Genesis. As a dedicated Christian and ardent creationist, Dan wants to use his God-given talents for the Lord's work. He not only is a very talented artist, but has a tremendous in-depth understanding of creation/evolution and Genesis. This enables him to capture complicated concepts and put them into picture form. Truly it could be said that each picture is worth a thousand words.

Printed in China

Please visit our website for other great titles:
www.masterbooks.net

How to Use This Multipurpose Family Book

1. Entertaining ABC Rhyme Book

You will fall in love with the Dodo bird. Everyone gets to watch this little character and his words of wisdom in this entertaining rhyme book. The first section consists of strikingly colorful illustrations, oftentimes very humorous, and a rhyme that teaches a very important foundational Biblical truth.

Younger children will enjoy just looking at the pictures and what they see tells it all! The whole Gospel message from Creation to the New Heaven and New Earth is obvious from the artwork alone. Older children, as well as adults, will enjoy reading the rhymes that go along with the drawings and they too will learn vital foundational truths.

Actually, the illustrations will speak to *all* age groups. Just look through the pages, and you will see what we mean!

2. Sunday School/Christian School/Home School/Home Devotional Teaching Book

The second part of this book contains notes for parents and teachers (and older children) that resembles a commentary on Genesis. Many unique concepts are discussed teaching the Gospel from Genesis and showing how foundational it is to the rest of Scripture.

At the end of the notes for each illustration, you will find student exercises that can be adapted for different age levels.

In the third part of the book, black and white drawings of each of the color illustrations shown in the first part of the book can be used for photocopying, etc. Feel free to copy these pictures and use them for hand-outs.

For teaching purposes, both the color illustrations and the black and white pictures can be made into overhead transparencies.

3. Coloring Book

The black and white pictures in the third section of the book can be colored by the children. This will help reinforce the Biblical concepts they learn as they read through the first part of the book. If you don't want the children drawing in the book, then you can photocopy the pages for them.

We are praying that not only will children and adults be better equipped to understand and defend the Gospel, but many will come to know the Savior as a result of this book.

We sincerely thank everyone who contributed suggestions as we put this publication together. We especially thank Dan Lietha for his long hours of painstaking work to produce the outstanding paintings that are featured in this publication.

Dedicated to Mervyn Ham
1928–1995

This book is dedicated to our Dad, Mervyn Ham, who went home to be with the Lord June 9, 1995. *A is for Adam* was produced because of the legacy he left us—a love for the Word of God. Our father never had great earthly riches, but he left his six children (and children's children) a spiritual inheritance more precious than silver or gold (Proverbs 13:22).

In his last hours, he told his family that life is all about "for and with." If you live in this world, it is *for* Christ and when you die it is *with* Christ. This book stands firm on the inerrancy and authority of Scripture while presenting the Gospel message to children and adults. It is our prayer that lives will be changed for the Lord so *many* will know what it means to be "for and with" as our precious Dad declared.

A is for **Adam**; God made him from dust.
He wasn't a monkey, he looked just like us.
Although some scientists don't think it was so,
It was God who was there, and He ought to know.

B is for **Bible**, a book God did give,
To tell where we came from and how we should live.
We did not evolve, God made it so plain,
People are people, we stay just the same.

___

C is for **Creatures**; God made them all,
Some rather little, but others quite tall.
He said unto Adam, "What names do you think?"
Adam then named them, quick as a wink!

D is for **Dinosaur**, Dodo and Deer,
Like all of the animals, no man did they fear.
But even though all was in true harmony,
Adam then realized, "There's no one like me!"

E is for **Eve**, his beautiful bride,
God made just for Adam, from part of his side.
To sleep God did put him, and when he awoke,
"She's flesh of my flesh," were the words that he spoke.

F is for **Fruit**, God said not to take,
"Because if you do, much trouble you'll make!"
They lived in the garden God specially made,
And if they'd obeyed Him, they could have then stayed.

G is for **Ghastly**, for what happened next,
Let's go to the Bible, and look at the text.
In Genesis chapter three and verse one,
Eve met the serpent, but she didn't run.

H is for **How** very sly he did sound,
The Devil saw Eve and the fruit she had found.
"Did God really say, 'Don't eat from that tree?'
It'll open your eyes—you'll be wise, like me."

I is for **Interested**, Eve did become,
She picked off the fruit and then she ate some.
It tasted so nice, what harm could there be?
"Here Adam, eat some and come and join me."

J is for **Jovial**, as Satan must have been,
The Devil was gleeful with all he had seen.
He was able to trick poor Eve with a lie,
"Obey all my words, and you'll surely not die!"

K is for **Knew**; Adam saw he was bare.
Both he and his wife no clothes they did wear.
They sewed up some fig leaves, and then tried to hide,
As they suddenly realized the Devil had lied.

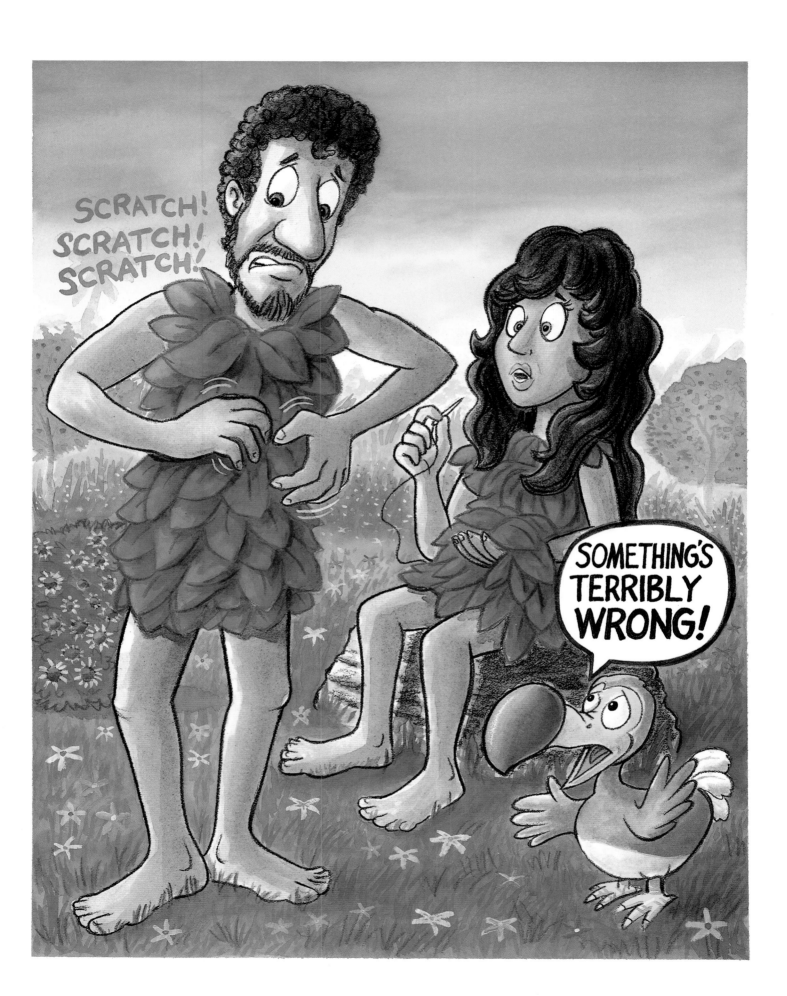

L is for **Lord**, who reigns up on high,
The One who told Adam, "Obey, or you'll die."
Adam and Eve couldn't hide from their sin,
"Out of my garden, and don't come back in!"

M is for **Moan**, what a mess sin did make.
Thorns, thistles and death, and
            cursed ground for man's sake.
God had to judge sin, He's so holy and pure,
But God is so good, He provided a cure.

N is for **Never**, no more could they go,
Back to the garden, where rivers did flow.
Angels with sword now stood at the gate,
What was in store, and what was their fate?

O is for **Offering**, an animal was killed.
Because of their sin, blood had to be spilled.
But over and over this had to be done,
Till Christ on the cross the victory had won.

P is for **Plan**, which God always had,
Because he knew man, would turn very bad.
A few thousand years later, God's Son came to be,
A wonderful Savior for you and for me.

Q is for **Quiet**, Adam and Eve must have been,
When God spoke the words, of
Genesis three verse fifteen.
God's Son came to die and be raised from the dead,
So to Hell we'd not go, but to Heaven instead.

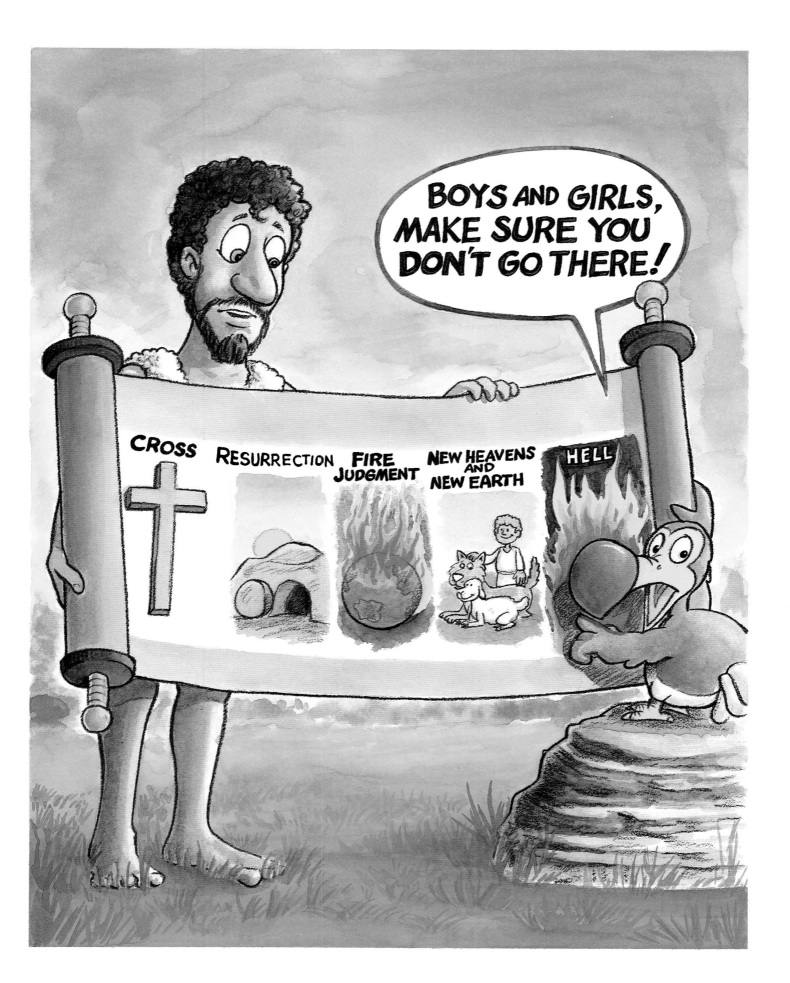

R is for **Rough**, how life had become,
The effects of God's curse had really begun.
Adam worked hard to obtain food to eat,
He made lots of sweat, so he must have been beat!

S is for **Seventy**, and maybe lots more,
Imagine their family with children galore.
Long before Moses, when people were few,
Brothers and sisters could marry, that's true!

T is for **Trouble**, OH!, such a sad day,
Cain struck brother Abel, and dead there he lay.
The Lord punished Cain for what he had done,
But things still got worse, there was much more to come.

U is for **Utterly** shocking and bad.
People were killing, it became quite a fad!
God said, "That's enough! The world I will judge."
He sent a great flood—which made lots of sludge.

V is for **Violent**, were the waters of the flood,
People and animals were buried in the mud.
But God saved Noah, wife, daughters and sons,
Along with the animals in an ark weighing tons.

W is for **Walk**; they came out of the ark.
The world was so different, the Flood left its mark.
Had people now learnt God's Word to obey?
They certainly did not, it is so sad to say.

X is in **eXplode**, the population sure grew,
But what happened next, read God's Word for the clue.
They built a great tower to reach to the sky,
For God's spoken Word, they were quick to defy.

Y is for **Yes**, God did soon judge their sin,
By confusing their language—what a terrible din!
He scattered the people all over the place,
Till God's final judgment, we'll all have to face.

Z is for **Zip**, so quick it will be,
When Jesus comes back for you and for me.
If our name is found in the ''Lamb's Book of Life,''
We'll sure live forever in a place with no strife.

A Genesis Commentary for Parents and Children

These notes are designed to give you the background information for each rhyme, thus equipping you to explain the concepts in greater detail. It is almost like reading a commentary on the book of Genesis.

Each sequence of verses teaches the Gospel message to children as well as answering such questions as:

How can we know we didn't evolve from monkeys?

Why do people get married?

Why do we wear clothes?

What did sin do to the world?

Where did Cain get his wife?

Why are there different languages?

How did the (so called) races of people come into existence?

How many different colors of humans are there?

Why is there death and suffering in the world?

Why did Jesus have to die?

How can we spend eternity in heaven with our Creator?

You will notice *A is for Adam* actually teaches the Bible chronologically. You will be teaching your children the time line of history beginning with Creation and ending with the New Heavens and New Earth. Everything we learn concerning the universe goes back to this time line. This foundational information is needed so the meaning of life (past, present and future) can be understood.

Along the way, the major events of history will be highlighted so children will comprehend the foundational truths necessary to understand Christianity. At the end of this walk through history, children will not only understand the Gospel, but they will know what they believe and why they believe it. They will then be better equipped to defend the Gospel and explain it to others.

As you teach this book, pray that the Lord will not only enable you to assure children of their salvation or lead them to Christ, but to also enable them to boldly defend their faith.

A is for **Adam**; God made him from dust.
He wasn't a monkey, he looked just like us.
Although some scientists don't think it was so,
It was God who was there, and He ought to know.

I CAN THINK, COMPOSE MUSIC, BUILD BRIDGES, FLY AIRPLANES, AND MAKE COMPUTERS !!!! WHAT CAN YOU DO?

Job 38:4 reminds us that only God has always been there. I Corinthians 8:1–3 tells us that compared to what God knows, human beings know nothing. Therefore, the only way to find out where we came from is to read the Word of God. Our Creator is the One who knows everything because He has always been there.

The Bible tells us that *all* things were created by and for Jesus Christ (Colossians 1:16). Genesis 1:26, 27 and 2:7 instruct us that God made the first man from the dust of the earth. God did *not* use any existing animal such as a monkey. He made it clear that the idea of evolution (that man evolved from some ape-like creature) does not fit with what the Bible tells us. Either the Bible is right—or evolution is right! Both cannot be true because what they say is *so* different.

Later, we will learn that because of sin Adam was told he would return to the dust from which he was made (Genesis 3:19). (When people die, their bodies return to dust—they do not return to some ape-like creature. Thus, the evolution story *cannot* be added to the Bible.)

Remember, the evolutionary scientists who tell us man evolved from some creature that looked like a monkey do not know everything, and were *not* there to see Creation happen. This is just *their* story—*their* belief.

Notice in the illustration that Adam is speaking, but the monkey is just thinking about a banana. The point is that Adam can speak—monkeys, apes and the like *cannot* speak. These creatures have no ability to speak. They were created very *different* from people.

Adam could speak as soon as he was created. In Genesis 1:28 we have the account of God speaking to Adam and Eve after they were created—they obviously understood every word. Genesis 2:20 tells us that Adam gave names to the animals. In Genesis 2:23, we read the first recorded words of Adam as he speaks about the woman God made for him.

One way to help children understand this is by using a computer. Explain to them that man makes a computer so that the finished product will carry out certain commands. Some computers even respond with words. For instance, you can now purchase a computer that reacts to your voice. You can say, "Windows please," and it will bring up the program.

However, computers can't talk like humans—they will only do what man has programmed them to do. If man can do this, we should have no trouble understanding how the infinite Creator, God, could create the brains of Adam and Eve already programmed with a language. Remember, Adam and Eve were not born as babies and then learned a language like we do today. These first two people were made as mature human beings—they had to teach their children the language God had given them.

It may also be important at this stage to point out that Genesis Chapter 1 is actually a summary in chronological order (six sequential days of creation) of all that God created. Genesis Chapter 2 gives specific details—particularly in relation to how He made Adam and Eve. These chapters are not contradictory, but *complementary* accounts. As we go through these rhymes, it will become obvious that the detailed events of Genesis Chapter 2 will be used to explain the summary given in Genesis Chapter 1.

People are very special. God made man in his own image, and breathed into man the breath of life (Genesis 1:27; Genesis 2:7).

Student Exercise:

Evolutionists indoctrinate us to think that apes and monkeys are very similar to us. Actually, if we did not grow up with this type of brainwashing, we would not think them to be similar nearly as much as we do. They are very different in many respects, though more similar to us than other creatures.

Have the children work from photographs, or preferably, go to a zoo; have them write down all the *differences* they see between animals such as apes and themselves. Then emphasize these differences. You can also mention there are some things that are similar—which is what we would expect from a common Creator. Instead, tell them that the differences show us clearly that we are *not* related to them.

Hint: Look for differences such as: apes cannot speak; their feet are more like hands; they may use a stick as a sort of tool, but they never use a tool to make a tool like humans can; they walk differently, etc.

B is for **Bible**, a book God did give,
To tell where we came from and how we should live.
We did not evolve, God made it so plain,
People are people, we stay just the same.

Genesis 1:26 states: "And God said, Let us make man in our image, after our likeness. . . ." In Genesis 2:7 we read: "And the Lord God formed man of the dust of the ground, and breathed into his nostrils the breath of life; and man became a living soul." We read in Genesis 2:21–22: "And the Lord God caused a deep sleep to fall upon Adam, and he slept: and he took one of his ribs, and closed up the flesh instead thereof: And the rib, which the Lord God had taken from man, made he a woman, and brought her unto the man."

Compare these verses to Genesis 1:24 which reads, "And God said, Let the earth bring forth the living creature after his kind, cattle, and creeping thing, and beast of the earth after his kind: and it was so."

Many generations ago, our first parents, Adam and Eve, were not made like the animals. It is very important for children to understand that they are *not* animals. Even though secular textbooks, television, nature programs, newspapers, public school curriculums, etc., state that man is an animal—it is imperative that children be taught the following:

1. Whereas God created the animals by commanding the earth to "bring forth the living creature. . ." (Genesis 1:24), Adam was made by God who specially formed him from the dust of the ground. God then breathed into Adam. Notice that God did not just command the dust to produce a man as He did for the animals—God himself formed man directly from dust. God did not breathe into the animals, but He certainly did for man. In other words, God imparted something special to the first man.

God also created the first woman by putting Adam to sleep and taking part of his side to form Eve. No animal was made this way. Only the human female was made *from* the human male.

You could also use this to show that there is no possibility that what the Bible states could in any way fit with the idea of evolution. Evolutionary theory teaches that chemicals evolved into the first life, and then after millions of years, some ape-like animal evolved into a human.

However, the Bible teaches that man was *not* made from some pre-existing animal, but from dust—this

58

does not fit with evolution at all. Not only this, but the first woman was made from the first man! She was made differently from the way man was made. According to evolution, the first human woman evolved from some pre-existing ape-like animal.

Thus, you can show children that one cannot believe in evolution and say that the Bible agrees with this! The record of the creation of man and woman as recorded in the Bible makes it clear that evolution is totally wrong.

2. Genesis 1:27 tells us that God made the first two humans in His own image. He did not do this for any of the animals—only humans. In other words, humans are very special. They are of far greater value than animals.

The Bible teaches that all humans will live forever, even after they die. Animals do not live forever. Once they die, that is the end of them. Ecclesiastes seems to say this when it tells us: "Who knoweth the spirit of man that goeth upward, and the spirit of the beast that goeth downward to the earth?" (Ecclesiastes 3:21).

Also, as we will learn later, Jesus Christ came to earth as a human so that He could die for all humans. None of the animals can be saved like we can.

Jesus, who is God, did **not** become an animal when He came to earth! He could become a man because man is made in God's image.

Animals cannot think like humans. People can think in an abstract way only because they are different from animals, being made in God's image.

Now we can certainly tell children that the body God created for human beings has similar characteristics to the mammals (e.g., hair, warm blooded, feed young on milk, etc.) However, man is in a category separate from that of the animals because he is **not** an animal.

Sadly, many people today (even Christians) have been indoctrinated to think of man as just an animal. Therefore, when a baby is developing in its mother's womb, they think it is just an animal also. As a result, many women who abort babies believe they are just getting rid of an animal—just as you would have a veterinarian put unwanted cats or dogs to sleep (in other words make them die).

If God is so concerned about this world and the animals that not even one sparrow can fall to the ground without his knowing it (Matthew 10:29), then how much more must He be concerned about His creatures that are made in His image? (Matthew 6:28–30).

We are even told that God's thoughts about us each day are more than we can count! (Psalm 139). Think about it. God thinks about each one of us all day long—but how often do we think about and talk to God during one day! So often we forget that God is there.

Teach the children that God is thinking about us every moment of the day. (For instance: Billy—God is thinking about you right now—and He is thinking about everyone else in the world right now too—Billy you are very special—all humans are very special.) We should be reminded to think about God and pray to Him as much as we can throughout the day. God wants us to talk to Him. (Psalm 139:17–18: "How precious also are thy thoughts unto me, O God! . . . If I should count them, they are more in number than the sand: when I awake, I am still with thee.")

Student Exercise

Have the children construct a chart to classify the creatures and plants God has created. Get them to put *three* headings: People, Animals, and Plants.

Underneath the "Animal" and "Plant" headings, have them list some of their favorites. Make sure they add apes and monkeys to the animal list.

Underneath the heading of "People," have them put Adam and Eve (first parents) and the names of some Bible characters (e.g., Noah, Shem, Job, Paul, Peter, etc.). Next, put their name at the bottom of the list. You could even have them put a photo of themselves and their favorite animals and plants.

At the top of the chart, have them print:

My name is _____.
I am made in God's image. I am not an animal.

At the bottom of the page, they can print:

I am very Special!

C is for **Creatures**; God made them all,
Some rather little, but others quite tall.
He said unto Adam, "What names do you think?"
Adam then named them, quick as a wink!

In Genesis 2:19–20, we read: "And out of the ground the Lord God formed every beast of the field, and every fowl of the air; and brought them unto Adam to see what he would call them: and whatsoever Adam called every living creature, that was the name thereof. And Adam gave names to the cattle, and to the fowl of the air, and to every beast of the field; . . ."

First, we need to make sure the children understand that the naming of the animals happened on the sixth day of Creation. We know this because we are told in Genesis Chapter 1 that on day six God created the land animals and Adam and Eve (Genesis 1:24–30).

Genesis Chapter 2 gives us more details about some of the events of Chapter 1. Here we are told that Adam gave names to the animals **before** Eve was made. Thus, the events of day six include:

1. God created the land animals (cattle, creeping things, beast & birds—Genesis 1:24–25).

2. God created Adam from dust (Genesis 2:7).

3. God put Adam in the Garden of Eden.

4. God warned Adam not to eat from the tree of the knowledge of good and evil, or he would die.

5. God brought the cattle, fowl, and beast for Adam to name (Genesis 2:19–20). Notice it does not list the creeping things—so it seems Adam did not name them.

6. Adam gave names to the animals.

Day six is continued in part "D."

In this section we are concerned primarily with Adam naming the animals. Now, this particular event is often used by people to claim that the days of Creation could not be six literal 24 hour days. These skeptics say that there is no way that Adam could have named all the animals during this time interval. Since God created the land animals first and then made Adam, obviously Adam had less than one day to name them. After he named them, then God made Eve.

So, on the surface it may seem like too much to accomplish in one day. However, we need to carefully consider the following:

1. How many animals did Adam have to name? For instance did he have to name a couple of hundred types of dogs? The answer is no! All our domestic dogs, as well as wolves, coyotes, dingoes etc., are all the **same kind** of animal—the dog kind. Notice that when God makes the animals, He makes them "after his kind"—(e.g., Genesis 1:24–25).

In other words, distinct **kinds** (or groups) of animals were made to reproduce after their **own** kind. This is actually another argument against evolution, which requires that one kind of animal change into another over millions of years.

Explain to the children that the fact that we have numerous varieties of dogs has nothing to do with evolution—they are still dogs! Just as God made Adam and Eve to have millions of descendants, including you and me, who all (unless they are identical twins) look a little different; so did He make the dog kind to produce dogs that all look a little different. This happens because of the enormous amount of information God put in the genes of our cells. This shows how great God is.

Therefore, in the Garden of Eden when Adam was naming the animals, he would not have had to name all the different types of bears—just bear kind. Thus, Adam would not have had to name nearly as many animals as we think.

By the way, the same is true for dinosaurs. Although there are hundreds of names for dinosaurs, there were probably fewer than fifty actual *kinds* of such creatures.

2. When God made Adam, he was not a baby—he was a mature human being. He did not have to learn to talk. Just as man today can program a computer so it can "sort of" talk. God, who is the infinite Creator, would have had no problem programming a language into Adam so he could talk with Him as soon as he was made.

   Today, every human being is born with the ability to talk, but has to be taught a language by his parents. For instance, Adam and Eve would have had to teach their children to talk—so who taught Adam and Eve to talk? God did. He would have made their brain with all the information for language already programmed in.

   This is why God could talk to Adam about not eating from the tree of the knowledge of good and evil or else he would die. Adam knew what this meant because he had the language programmed in his brain that God had given him.

   So, Adam would have had no problem giving names to the animals.

3. Would Adam have had enough time to give the names though? We need to be careful in thinking about this. You see, usually we think this way, "Well, I couldn't do all that in less than a day, so how could Adam?"

   The point is that the Bible tells us that we have all suffered the effects of six thousand years of the curse because of sin. Adam was perfect when he was made—he would have had a perfect memory—he was very intelligent indeed.

   It would have been easy for Adam to think of a name and remember it immediately. This should help us understand what sin has done to the world. Man is not getting better as evolutionists tell us—we are all running down, degenerating because of sin. That is why we look forward to our new bodies when Jesus comes back to take those who love Him to heaven.

   Incidentally, the artist put something very subtle into this illustration. Look under Adam's right arm, just above the creature that looks like a wolf. You should see a small gray tail—the tail of the hippo. What is the significance of this? Notice the Behemoth (from Job 40:15) in this picture. We have pictured Behemoth as a dinosaur, as the description from Job 40 fits this animal. We are told that

Behemoth moved his tail like a "cedar tree." Some Bible commentaries say that Behemoth was an elephant or hippopotamus, but compare the hippo tail to that of Behemoth! The hippo tail does *not* fit the description of Job 40.

Student Exercise

Research project: Go to a library and look up the *Guiness Book of Records*. Look for examples of people with photographic memories who can do large calculations without a calculator, can do great physical feats, or who are brilliant musicians, artists, etc.

Get the children to draw a picture of Adam (or photocopy the picture for "C"), and then list somewhere on the page the various talents they discovered from the *Guiness Book of Records* that people possess. They could draw a line from each talent to Adam's head (brain). Explain that Adam could have done all of this plus much, much more. If people today can do such marvelous feats, just imagine how much the first perfect man could have done.

Another example you could use to help children understand this is the memory of a computer. Show them that as soon as we type the information in a computer and put it into the "memory banks," we can recall it at any time.

Now man's brain is much, much, *much* more complicated than the most intricate computer. If man can make a computer with a memory and man is made by God, then obviously God can make man's computer (the brain) to be so much better than the best manmade computer. The problem, though, is that man's brain suffers from the effects of sin. It is no longer a perfect computer, and it doesn't function as well as it used to.

D is for **Dinosaur**, Dodo and Deer,
Like all of the animals, no man did they fear.
But even though all was in true harmony,
Adam then realized, "There's no one like me!"

Note: The Dodo bird first appeared in "C." From now on you will notice the Dodo bird making statements to help children get the point of the rhyme and the picture.

Children need to understand that the Dodo bird cannot think or speak like humans. The reason we chose a Dodo bird is that it is believed to be extinct. This helps make an important point later on.

In "A," we learned that apes and other animals cannot speak. They are made quite different from humans. However, we needed a character to make some comments (sometimes quite humorous) to help teach important concepts to children. Since children are familiar with cartoons and know that animals really can't speak or think like humans, we decided that we could ask the children to imagine what the Dodo bird might say if he *could* speak.

The children will look forward to seeing what the Dodo bird is doing in each picture. In fact, we want them to identify with the Dodo. In other words, looking from the outside in, this is what they would have said if they were there watching these events. This is also meant to help children think about situations and ask the right questions.

In a teaching situation, if you are reading this book to children for the first time, cover up what the Dodo says and ask the children to guess from the picture what it might be saying.

Following on from "C," we read the rest of Genesis 2:20, ". . . but for Adam there was not found an help meet for him."

More of the activities of day six of the Creation week include: see "C" for points 1–6.

7. Adam realized that the animals consisted of male and female—they all had mates. However, Adam did not have a mate. Notice in the cartoon picture for "D" the question the Dodo bird asks, "Where's Mrs. Adam?

You can again use this information to teach against evolution. When Adam looked around, he would have seen monkeys as well as various other creatures. However, there was not one creature he saw that was anything like him. Adam certainly did not think that a monkey was anything like a human being. He recognized that he did not have a mate.

This also means there were *no* other humans. Some people have tried to say that God created other people, and this is where Cain obtained his wife. We will learn later that *all* humans go back to only two people; if this were not so, then the whole Gospel message fails since *only* descendants of Adam and Eve can be saved. Thus, when Adam looked around, he saw *no* other humans—no one that could be suitable as a mate for him.

It is also clear that God wanted Adam to understand that his mate was not made at the same time as he. We will learn that God made Eve *from* Adam. Also, the fact that Adam was created first is confirmed by Paul in 1 Timothy 2:13 concerning the headship of the man in marriage. It would be good to have the children look up this verse so they can see that Paul, a New Testament writer, obviously believed the events of Genesis concerning the creation of Adam as Eve as literal, historical events.

Impress upon the children that originally all of the animals were not frightened of Adam or each other. Adam was certainly not fearful of the animals. Everything was in true harmony. Read Genesis 9:2 to show the children that the animals were not fearful of man until after the flood. We will learn that this change occurred because of sin.

Point out that the harmony they see in this picture is not the harmony we see today. Obviously, something has happened to change the world. Tell them we are going to learn about what did happen and why the world is not in harmony today.

You could also have the children look up Isaiah 11:6-9. This passage tells us of a *future* time when the animals and man will all be in harmony again. Explain that this description fits with the picture they see in "D." It also means that in addition to learning what happened to change the harmony that once existed, something else has happened so that this harmony will exist once again in the future.

We like to put it this way: In the future, "the wolf also shall dwell with the lamb . . ." which is how it was *originally*. However, today, the lamb "dwells" *in* the wolf—some animals, including man, now eat other animals.

Make sure the children also recognize the dinosaurs beside Adam. This is to reinforce the fact that dinosaurs lived with people, since they were also made on the sixth day—the same day that Adam and Eve were created.

Student Exercise

Have the children pretend they are Adam in the garden with all the animals, but with no other humans. Get them to look up the meaning of the word "lonely" in a dictionary. They can then write a page essay on what it would have been like for Adam to be lonely. Imagine, you are the only human in the world— you are all alone—how would you feel? Would you be sad? Would you be perplexed? Remember though, Adam was perfect—he had not sinned yet, so his thoughts would not have been sinful thoughts.

Next, talk to the children about people who are lonely today. Perhaps you could organize a visit to a rest home or go to see some lonely people. Teach the children that God's Word tells us to help others who are lonely and in need (Matthew 25:34–36,40; Luke 14:13–14).

E is for **Eve**, his beautiful bride,
God made just for Adam, from part of his side.
To sleep God did put him, and when he awoke,
"She's flesh of my flesh," were the words that he spoke.

A climax of the activities of Day Six was the creation of the first woman:

8. God put Adam to sleep and made Eve from his side.

9. God made the very first marriage. Note that Genesis 2:24 is used in Matthew 19:4–5 and Ephesians 5:31 as being foundational to the teaching of the marriage relationship of one man for one woman for life.

Genesis 2:21–22 states: "And the Lord God caused a deep sleep to fall upon Adam, and he slept: and He took one of his ribs, and closed up the flesh instead thereof: And the rib, which the Lord God had taken from man, made he a woman, and brought her unto the man."

This is the first operation ever performed on a human! God took part of Adam's side and made the first woman.

Help the children understand that Adam did not *see* God make Eve, and Eve did not see God make anything—everything was completed by this time. In other words, both Adam and Eve had to believe God's Word—they had to have faith.

Now Adam knew that there was no one in the world like him. But when he awoke after God put him to sleep, there was his beautiful mate. He knew God had made her. Obviously, God told Adam how He made Eve so he could understand that she was made from him. How special, his mate was made from his own bone and flesh.

It is important to help the children understand that none of us saw God make the world or the animals, and we too must have faith that God did it just like we are told in His Word, the Bible. Sadly, a lot of people today don't want to believe God's Word. They want to believe a story (evolution) made up by people who weren't there to see the world and animals have a beginning. The point is, God has always been there and knows everything. Therefore, we should trust the Word of God—not the word of men. This is something we are warned about in the Bible over and over again. Psalm 118:8 states: "It is better to trust in the Lord than to put confidence in man."

However, our faith is *not* a blind faith. We can use our minds to see that the evidence fits the Bible.

For instance, we are told that God made distinct *kinds* of animals and plants—and that is what we see. We do *not* see one *kind* of animal changing into another as evolutionists would teach us. The evidence around us fits with the Bible—not with evolution.

Also, the Bible tells us that God made Adam from dust. Thus, Adam and Eve's bodies (and therefore ours because we are their descendants) must have been made from the elements of the earth. We know this is true, because when a person dies, his body returns to dust.

We read on in Genesis 2:22–24: "And the rib, which the Lord God had taken from man, made he a woman, and brought her unto the man. And Adam said, This is now bone of my bones, and flesh of my flesh: she shall be called Woman, because she was taken out of Man. Therefore shall a man leave his father and his mother, and shall cleave unto his wife: and they shall be one flesh."

Have the children learn the *first recorded* words of Adam in Genesis 2:23. Obviously, at this time, Adam had already given names to the animals. Isn't it significant that these words were spoken about his wife Eve? She was to be his mate for life (just as all marriages should be), and she was to be the mother of all human beings—other than Adam. Later, we will be considering Genesis 3:20 in greater detail ("And

Adam called his wife's name Eve, because she was the mother of all living").

It is important here that you introduce the doctrine of marriage. Explain that this is where marriage comes from because God made the first marriage. Tell the children that just as Eve was part of Adam and made specially for Adam to be his mate for life, so too when a man and woman get married today they should be together for life.

Make the point that in today's world there are people who believe that two men or two women can get married. Point out that when God made marriage, He made a man and a woman—*not* two men or two women. Show them from Matthew 19:4–5 that Jesus, the One who made the world and created all things (Colossians 1:16), quoted from this section of Genesis.

This has two very important implications:

1. Jesus Christ, who is God, believed the words in the book of Genesis to be true. Therefore we should believe them.

2. Jesus showed that the doctrine of marriage is built upon these events of Genesis. That is why it is *wrong* for a man to marry a man, or a woman to marry a woman.

You can also show them that Paul quoted from this section of Genesis in Ephesians 5:31. Paul too believed the words of Genesis.

One of the questions often asked by people concerns the "rib" of Adam. If God really took a rib to make Eve, then the question is asked, "Wouldn't men have one less rib than a woman?" To answer this question, consider someone who had an accident and sadly had to have their leg amputated. If they had children later, would they all have one leg missing? Of course not. It is the information in our genes that determines how our body is built. The information in Adam's genes for the number of ribs that he had did not change. His children would have the same number with which he was created.

Student Exercise

Have the children look up the following New Testament passages. Ask them to see if they can find the section in Genesis containing these passages. Help them to understand that what is written in the New Testament is dependent upon the book of Genesis being true. Also, help them understand how important it is to believe that the book of Genesis is the only totally true and reliable history book in the world, and this is because it is the Word of God. He alone knows everything and has always been there.

This exercise is important because many Christians think that Genesis, particularly the first eleven chapters, is just myth or symbolic. However, if those chapters were just myth, then the rest of the Bible could mean anything since it is really founded upon Genesis 1:1–11. If Genesis is just myth, then perhaps the writings of the New Testament are just myth also since many times the text refers back to the events in Genesis.

Children should understand from this exercise that Genesis is a record of actual history, and the New

Testament writers along with the Old Testament writers believed this to be so.

New Testament Passages

2 Peter 3:4–7	1 Corinthians 11:8–9
Mark 10:6–7	Revelation 22:14
Matthew 19:4–5	2 Corinthians 11:3
1 Timothy 2:12–14	Romans 8:21–22
Exodus 20:11	Romans 5:12
Ephesians 5:30–31	Matthew 24:37–39

(**Note**: These are just a few of over 200 such references)

F is for **Fruit**, God said not to take,
"Because if you do, much trouble you'll make!"
They lived in the garden God specially made,
And if they'd obeyed Him, they could have then stayed.

Have the children look up Genesis 2:9:

"And out of the ground made the Lord God to grow every tree that is pleasant to the sight, and good for food; the tree of life also in the midst of the garden, and the tree of knowledge of good and evil."

Then read Genesis 2:16–17:

"And the Lord God commanded the man, saying, Of every tree of the garden thou mayest freely eat: But of the tree of the knowledge of good and evil, thou shalt not eat of it: for in the day that thou eatest thereof thou shalt surely die."

Have the children think about how many trees God may have made—maybe millions. Adam and Eve would have had lots and lots of trees from which they could eat the fruit. There was only *one* tree from which they were forbidden to eat.

Why did God test Adam and Eve this way? If you have a puppet, use it to explain to the children that you can make the puppet do whatever you want. You control the puppet. Explain that God did not make Adam and Eve to be puppets. He did not make them and then force them to love and obey Him. God

wanted Adam and Eve to love Him because they wanted to. They had the ability to choose.

If you think about it, since God had made so many trees and told Adam and Eve that there was only one —just one—that they couldn't eat from. God really made it easy for Adam to show that they wanted to love and obey their Creator. In fact, God really made it hard for them to disobey. He put so many trees around them that must have had lovely fruit, and were "pleasant to look at"—that they would have had to go out of their way to eat from the one tree they were told to avoid.

Have the children look at the picture and take note of what the Dodo bird is saying. There is a strong hint here that something is going to happen that will affect the Dodo bird. Scientists believe the Dodo bird is extinct. This means it must have died, and as we have already indicated in other sections, death was the penalty for disobeying God.

Look back at the Bible passage at the beginning of this section. God told Adam that if he ate the forbidden fruit he would "die." Because we see death all around us in this present world, even without reading the rest of the account in Genesis, we should be able to guess that Adam *did* eat the forbidden fruit.

Some people say that the world before sin did not have any death (of animals or man), and Adam would not have known what God meant when he warned, "Thou shalt surely die." However, remember that when God made Adam He put into his brain all the information for him to have a language so he would have known the meaning of every word in the language. If God hadn't, Adam would not have been able to talk to God about anything. Even though he had not seen animals or humans die, he knew exactly what God meant as he had a perfect language right from the start.

The forbidden fruit was located on the "tree of knowledge of good and evil." Since the penalty for eating this fruit was to be death, we could really call this the "*tree of death.*"

The other special tree that God talked about was called the "tree of life." Notice that God did not tell them they could not eat from this tree. Its fruit was freely available to Adam and Eve. While they had access to this tree, it meant that they could live forever.

It is important to explain to the children that there was really nothing "magical" about these trees. The fruit would not have necessarily made Adam die or live forever. However, God had said that one was the "tree of life," and as long as God let Adam and Eve have the fruit from this tree, He would enable them to live forever. If Adam ate of the other special tree, "of the knowledge of good and evil," then God had determined that this was really the "tree of death." This meant that if Adam and Eve ate from this tree, God would cause them to die. To accomplish this, they had to be banished from the garden so they could not access the "tree of life."

Note that these two trees were in the special garden God had made (Genesis 2:8). Ask the children to think about what God would have to do if Adam ate the forbidden fruit. This would mean that God, who can not go back on His word, would have to make Adam and Eve die. This would also mean that they would no longer eat from the tree of Life. What would God have to do? When we get to "L," we will find out.

Have the children look up Genesis 2:16. Ask them who was given the command not to eat the forbidden fruit—was it Adam or Eve? This is very important, because as we will learn later, it is Adam who gets the blame. He was the one who was given the responsibility to ensure that the forbidden fruit was not eaten.

Notice in the illustration that the forbidden fruit is *not* an apple. The Bible does not tell us what kind of fruit it was, so our illustrator made it look different from any fruit we know of today.

Student Exercise

Have the children read this short story, and then answer the questions.

One Day, Mr. Ham talked with his son Jeremy about what was in their refrigerator.

"Jeremy!"

"Yes Dad."

"Jeremy, in the refrigerator, there are lots of nice chocolates, but there is one special one that you are not to eat, it's mine."

"OK Dad."

Later that day, Jeremy looked in the refrigerator. There were lots of chocolates, but there was one that looked really, really nice. It was a special one—the one that Dad had said not to eat. It did look especially nice!

What do you think Jeremy did?

Why do you think he did this?

Who else is like this?

Why are they like this?

G is for **Ghastly**, for what happened next,
Let's go to the Bible, and look at the text.
In Genesis chapter three and verse one,
Eve met the serpent, but she didn't run.

This is the place where we introduce the serpent. When the children see the serpent illustrated in G, H, I & J, they should think of this creature as the Devil. Now who is the Devil? In Revelation 12:9 we read, "And the great dragon was cast out, that old serpent, called the Devil, and Satan, which deceiveth the whole world: he was cast out into the earth, and his angels were cast out with him."

He was made a very beautiful angel with great intelligence. Read Ezekiel 28:13–19. However, Satan did not want to accept his position as a created angel (Read Colossians 1:16 which tells us that Jesus Christ made *all* things). Isaiah 14:13 states: "For thou hast said in thine heart, I will ascend into heaven, I will exalt my throne above the stars of God: I will sit also upon the mount of the congregation, in the sides of the north." It appears Satan wanted to be like God and thought that he could become a god.

Perhaps Satan did not believe he was created. Maybe he thought he could "evolve" to be a god. When he was created, he was very special. However, Ezekiel tells us, "Thou wast perfect in thy ways from the day that thou was created, till iniquity was found in thee"(Ezekiel 28:15).

In John 8:44, we read that Satan is a liar. The Bible warns us that the Devil ". . . as a roaring lion, walketh about, seeking whom he may devour:" (1 Peter 5:8).

Now we have to explain how the serpent could talk! The Bible does not tell us much concerning the nature of this animal or how Satan used it to talk to Eve. Have the children look up Numbers 22 and read the story of Balaam's ass. In verse 28, we are told that God "opened the mouth of the ass"—in other words God used the ass to speak to Balaam.

Somehow, Satan used the serpent (whatever kind of animal it was then) to speak to Eve. Explain to the children that God does not explain *everything* to us. If He did, we would have an infinite number of books! We would never be able to read them. God provides

us with enough information for all we need to know. Help the children to not be concerned that we understand *all* of the details.

As we read through the Bible, we know that the Devil used the serpent to tempt Eve to disobey God's Word concerning the forbidden fruit.

Genesis 3:1 tells us that the serpent approached the woman (Eve). Why did he approach Eve and not Adam? Perhaps it was that Adam was the one to whom God commanded not to eat the forbidden fruit (Genesis 2:16–17). He was the one to whom God had spoken directly, and thus, he was given the responsibility.

In 1 Timothy 2:13, we are told that Adam was created first, which is one of the reasons he was to be the head of his household.

Adam, of course, would have told Eve what God had said. In Genesis 3:3, Eve states that she must not eat or touch the fruit. Adam probably had told her God's words about not eating the fruit, and then, to help his wife, told her not to even touch it because that might tempt her.

We can all think of examples where we want something but are not allowed. However, if we keep looking at it or touching it, we are more likely to be tempted to take it!

The rhyme tells us that Eve did not run. She stayed and listened to the Devil. She seemed to be attracted to the serpent. The Bible does tell us in the passages mentioned above that the serpent was beautiful. We have to be careful of this today because Satan will make that which he wants us to do look beautiful. But as we learn more about what happened to Adam and

Eve, we will see that there are terrible consequences when we don't obey God's Word.

How can we protect ourselves from the Devil today? How can we be sure we are not going to be attracted to what he says?

The following exercise will answer these questions.

Student Exercise

Read Ephesians 6:10–18. Draw a picture of yourself (or use a photograph). Next, draw each piece of God's armor mentioned in this passage and put it on your picture in the place it should go.

Commit this passage to memory. This will help you to always remember that if you know God's Word and obey what He says, you will be able to recognize when the Devil is trying to tempt you. This will enable you to fight him.

Also read Psalm 119:9–16. You can also write out verse 11.

H is for **How** very sly he did sound,
The Devil saw Eve and the fruit she had found.
"Did God really say, 'Don't eat from that tree?'
It'll open your eyes—you'll be wise, like me."

Read Genesis 3:1 carefully: "Now the serpent was more subtle than any beast of the field which the Lord God had made. And he said unto the woman, Yea, hath God said, Ye shall not eat of every tree of the garden?"

What was the Devil really asking Eve? He was actually saying, "Did God *really* say not to eat of all the trees?" Notice that he did not quote correctly what God had said. God had told Adam and Eve not to eat of only *one* tree. Satan was trying to make Eve think that God was unfair. It was also a trick to get Eve to answer him—which she did. Now he had started a conversation with her, which is exactly what he wanted.

Satan then started to question God's Word. He told Eve that she would *not* die if she ate from the tree. This, of course, was opposite to that which God had so clearly stated. He tried to convince Eve that God was not telling her everything. He told her that she could be like God (Genesis 3:5).

Imagine that a beautiful creature told you that you could be like God—so powerful! Eve must have listened intently. The Devil sounded so wise—he seemed to know more than she did. She became very curious.

In the illustration, you will notice the Dodo bird is crying out "No Eve! No!!" Just imagine, if we were watching there in the garden, that is what we would say because we now know what a dreadful thing it was that Eve did. If we had been Eve, we would have done the same thing. Because we are all children of Adam and Eve, we have inherited their nature. We are just like them. We shouldn't look at Eve and think what a terrible person she was and that we would not have done that! Actually, we would do exactly what she did. We are no different.

Because of all that God has revealed in his Word, we know the terrible consequences because Eve listened to the serpent.

2 Corinthians 11:3 states: "But I fear, lest by any means, as the serpent beguiled Eve through his subtilty, so your minds should be corrupted from the simplicity that is in Christ."

Paul is warning that Satan is going to use the same method with us as he did with Eve to stop us from believing God's Word. This is a warning that everyone should take very seriously.

Let's look again at the method Satan used to get Eve to disobey God's Word. Satan said "Yea, hath God said? . . . " In other words, "Did God really say that?" What was Satan doing? He was trying to get Eve to doubt God's Word—to doubt that she needed to believe every word that God had spoken.

Paul warns us that Satan is going to use this same method with us today, trying to get us not to believe the Word of God.

Explain to the children that there are many people today, even in churches, who don't believe God's Word, especially the book of Genesis. Satan has tempted these people like this: "Did God really say six days?. . . Did God really say global Flood? . . . Did God really say He made the first man from dust? . . . Did God *really* say these things?"

Explain to the children that today many Christians don't believe Genesis. They think that the days might be millions of years and not days, as it states. They believe that Noah's Flood might have only been a local event, not a worldwide event which the Bible clearly teaches. Some even think God must have made man from a monkey—but the Bible says he was made from dust!

If Satan has been so clever in getting people to disbelieve God's Word, just as he did with Eve, then he will try this with us as well. That is one reason we need to put on all of our "armor" as we learned in G.

Explain to the children that if they start to doubt that God's Word is true in Genesis, the first book, then this may result in their doubting the rest of the Bible.

Psalm 119:160 states that, "Thy word is true from the beginning:"

Once we doubt something, we may ultimately disbelieve it altogether.

Student Exercise

Look at the illustration. Notice that the serpent is wearing sunglasses. If you look at the illustration for J, the sunglasses are now missing.

Have the children write down the reason they think the serpent is wearing sunglasses.

Does Satan try to hide his true nature from us today? Look up 2 Corinthians 11:14.

Hint: Satan did not want Eve to know who he really was.

I is for **Interested**, Eve did become,
She picked off the fruit and then she ate some.
It tasted so nice, what harm could there be?
"Here Adam, eat some and come and join me."

R ead Genesis 3:6: "And when the woman saw that the tree was good for food, and that it was pleasant to the eyes, and a tree to be desired to make one wise, she took of the fruit thereof, and did eat, and gave also unto her husband with her; and he did eat."

Satan managed to get her to believe his lies. She longed for the fruit. She wanted to be "wise" like the serpent. She took the fruit and ate it.

Obviously nothing terrible happened to her. She did not die. She felt all right. Therefore, she must have believed even more that she needed this fruit.

When Adam saw that Eve had eaten the fruit, what do you think he *should* have done? Who had given him the command *not* to eat of it? Adam should have immediately gone to God and said, "We have a problem. This woman you made for me has eaten the forbidden fruit. Can you please tell me what to do?" However, Adam did not go to God with the problem. In fact, remember in "D," we learned that Adam was lonely and couldn't find a mate. God then made Eve from Adam's side. Adam would not have wanted to lose his mate. He wanted her to be his partner; after all, she was made *from* him. He must have seen that nothing terrible happened to her, so maybe he thought it was all right to eat the fruit also.

On the other hand, perhaps Adam realized what Eve had done. He may have understood that something terrible would happen to her; but since she was made from him, he decided to join her because he couldn't bear being without her. We don't know what went through Adam's mind. But we do know what he should have done, don't we? Adam should have gone to the One who made him, the all powerful creator God, and asked him for a solution. However, he did not do this.

Explain to the children that we are just like Adam. There are lots of times when we forget to ask God to help us in situations, and we try to do it in our own strength and get into trouble.

God promises that when we call upon Him, He *will* answer. He may not always answer the way we want, but He hears and answers every prayer. (Psalm 91:15; Isaiah 58:9; Luke 11:9; John 15:7).

We are commanded to spend time in prayer: "Pray without ceasing" (1 Thessalonians 5:17); "Praying always with all prayer and supplication in the Spirit, and watching thereunto with all perseverance and supplication for all saints" (Ephesians 6:18).

Now read Genesis 3:7: "And the eyes of them both were opened. . . ." It was after Adam ate the forbidden fruit that things began to happen because it was Adam who had been given the command directly from God not to eat from that tree. Adam was the head of this first marriage. He was responsible. This is the reason that in the New Testament we read that Adam is blamed for sin: "Wherefore, as by one man sin entered into the world, and death by sin; and so death passed upon all men, for that all have sinned" (Romans 5:12). As you read through Romans 5 and I Corinthians 15, it is always Adam who gets the blame for sin, not Eve.

From now on terrible things start to happen as a consequence of Adam's disobedience. The Bible calls this disobedience *sin*. Explain to the children that sin is being disobedient to God's Word. It is also important to understand that if these events of Genesis were not literal historical events, there would not have been a literal Fall. Thus, if there was no literal rebellion, then what is sin?

Sadly, many clergy today say that this story in Genesis is not real. They say it is just a myth or it's symbolic. If these events were not true, then the whole reason Jesus died on the cross (because of sin) becomes meaningless. Please refer to the book, *The Lie: Evolution* by Ken Ham, for more details concerning this important matter.

Sometimes children ask what would have happened if Adam had not sinned. Look up Revelation 13:8; this verse tells us that Christ was slain from the foundation of the world. Also consider Hebrews 9:26 and Ephesians 1:4. The point is, Adam was going to sin—God is all knowing. He knew what was going to happen.

Explain to the children that God knew what was going to happen and how terrible sin and death would be. He knew that Jesus would have to die on a cross to save us—and yet He still created us. How much He must love us!

Student Exercise

Give the children a chocolate to eat. Tell them to describe what it is like to eat the chocolate. It is sweet. It tastes nice. It makes me feel good, etc.

Now ask them to remember the short story about Jeremy in "F." If Jeremy took the special chocolate, would it have tasted sweet? But when Dad found out, what do you think might have happened to Jeremy?

Explain to them that sin often seems sweet like the chocolate, but afterward the results hurt us terribly. Ask them to write a short story about a boy or girl who disobey their parents. It seems such fun to them, but later, something happens for which they are very sorry. Help them to understand that sin can seem sweet, but it soon turns sour.

J is for **Jovial**, as Satan must have been,
The Devil was gleeful with all he had seen.
He was able to trick poor Eve with a lie,
"Obey all my words, and you'll surely not die!"

These notes also apply to the rhyme for "K."

The serpent has his sunglasses off. Now that he was able to get Adam and Eve to accept his word instead of God's Word, there is no need to hide his true nature. The damage has been done.

Adam was given dominion by God over Creation (Genesis 1:28). Now that Adam had accepted the word of the Devil, he had really given his allegiance to him.

The vital issue in this whole account concerns *death*. God had told Adam that if he disobeyed and ate the forbidden fruit he would "surely die" (Genesis 2:17). Actually, the Hebrew here literally means "dying, you will die."

The big lie of Satan was ". . . Ye shall not surely die" (Genesis 3:4).

Remember we learned that Adam must have noticed that Eve did not die when she ate the fruit, and that after Adam ate, things started to happen. They realized they were naked (Genesis 3:7)—they hid from God (Genesis 3:8). Something was happening to Adam and Eve. They obviously did not have the beautiful relationship with their Creator that they had before they sinned.

This can be called spiritual death. Their beautiful relationship with the God of the universe "died." But this was not the only "death" because of sin. In Genesis 5:5, we read these very sad words about Adam: ". . . and he died." It took 930 years, but his body died.

You see, when God had warned Adam about death, He had told them that "dying, you will die." This is exactly what happened. As soon as they sinned, they died spiritually; and then immediately started to die physically.

In Genesis 3:22–23, we read that God sent Adam and Eve out of the garden so they could not have access to the tree Of life. Otherwise, they would have been able to live forever in their sinful state. That would have been terrible.

Most children today are well aware that the world is a terrible place. We have seen all sorts of atrocities, bloodshed, violence, and wars. Explain that they are looking at the effects of sin. Imagine if all the worst people in the world like Hitler, Stalin and so on were able to live forever in this world—what a terrible place it would be!

Now comes the big question. Why did God bring such a horrible thing as death into the world? Actually, this is one of the most asked questions in today's world—"Why is there death and suffering in the world, if God is a God of love?"

Charles Darwin, who popularized the modern view of evolution, had a real problem with death. He could not believe there was a God of love because of all the death and suffering he saw around him. He was particularly angry about this when one of his beloved children died. Is there an answer? Well, the reason there is death and suffering in the world is because God *is* a God of love.

Explain to the children that God is holy—He is pure—He is without sin (Hebrews 4:15; 9:28). As you read the events recorded in Exodus, Leviticus, Numbers & Deuteronomy, you will start to grasp how holy God is.

God is so holy and so pure that any sinful human could not be in His presence. When God made Adam, this first man was perfect. He had a perfect relationship with God. However, because Adam rebelled against his Creator, he could no longer live in the presence of God. He really forfeited his right to live.

God caused Adam and Eve, and subsequently all their descendants to die physically. This was a righteous punishment because the first man had totally rebelled against his Creator. But even though all humans would die physically, their souls would live forever. Unfortunately, they could never live with God because they were sinners. (Animals do not have immortal souls, so in the fallen world because of death, they cease to exist.)

But God provided a solution for Adam and Eve and their descendants. Because Adam, the representative head of the entire human race (all humans are descendants of Adam and Eve), brought sin and death into the world, there needed to be a new Adam. This Adam would be the new representative head of the human race who would pay the penalty for sin.

This is where we discover the most wonderful message of all. God sent His son, the Lord Jesus Christ, Creator of all things, to be a perfect man. In I Corinthians 15:45, Paul calls Jesus the "last Adam." In other words, God provided another Adam. This perfect Adam (a descendant of Adam, thus a man, but born of a Virgin—a perfect man), suffered the curse of death on the cross paying for *all* our sins. He then rose from the dead, conquering death, so those who love and trust Him as their Savior can live forever *with* God instead of separated from Him. Do you realize that God Himself suffered the same judgment He placed on the world? He really must love us!

Of course, we will understand more about this as we go on. Even though Satan tricked Adam and Eve, God had already worked out a wonderful plan so everyone would have the opportunity of living with God for ever. This is a very important issue. Many Christians say that physical death has been in the world for millions of years, because of their belief that the fossil record is millions of years old. However, accepting this belief destroys the meaning of death and the reason that Jesus died on the cross. We will learn more about the inconsistencies of death before sin in coming sections.

When people believe in death and disease before sin (as people who believe in millions of years do), they are really trying to blame God for sickness and death instead of blaming *our* sin!

Remind the children again about keeping their "armor" on, as Satan will use all kinds of tricks to get them to disobey God. Satan wants everyone to obey

him, not our Creator. The Dodo bird is warning them to quickly turn the page to emphasize how we should shun the Devil's tricks when he uses them to try to get us to rebel.

Remind them that in "H" we learned that Satan is going to use the same "tricks" with us as he did on Adam and Eve. We need to always be aware of this.

Student Exercise

Look up the following verses of Scripture and write down the phrase that is common to all of them:

Genesis 5:5; 5:8; 5:11; 5:14; 5:17; 5:20; 5:27; 5:31; 9:29; 25:18.

Print this phrase in large letters on the top of a poster, and then draw a picture that you think best illustrates this phrase.

K is for **Knew**; Adam saw he was bare.
Both he and his wife no clothes they did wear.
They sewed up some fig leaves, and then tried to hide,
As they suddenly realized the Devil had lied.

When the Dodo bird comments here that "something's terribly wrong," he is pointing to the fact that Adam and Eve sewed fig leaves together for clothes because they saw they were naked (Genesis 3:7). Actually, this tells you something about Adam and Eve's intelligence. Can you sew fig leaves together and make "aprons" (clothes)? Obviously Adam and Eve were naked before sin, and this was not a problem at all, but sin changes everything. Children must be aware of this. We will learn in "O" that God gave Adam and Eve clothes—but special clothes as we will discover.

Today, there are people who say there is nothing wrong with taking their clothes off anywhere. You can see nudity on some beaches, and on television. Some people say that because we are born naked, it is "natural" to go around without clothes. What they are ignoring is *sin*. Sin changed everything, and that is the lesson we need to instill in our children.

Surely by now, Adam and Eve must have realized that something was terribly wrong. I am sure they began to understand that the serpent had not told them the truth. They were still alive, so the reality of death had not really hit them. But later, when they see the dead body of their son, Abel, it must have been very distressing to them.

Now, Adam and Eve would start to grow old, and they would begin to change. It is sad for us to see people getting old and dying. It must have been terrible for Adam and Eve to realize that all their descendants would now suffer the judgment of death because of sin. In a way, one of the reasons they tried to make clothes was to cover up their sin. They realized they were naked and wanted to cover up so they wouldn't feel so bad.

Student Exercise

Ask your parents to obtain a medical book from the library that contains information concerning the many diseases that humans can get. Have them go through this book with you and list several of these. While you are doing this, think about the fact that *all* of these diseases and many more came into the world because of sin.

This should help us understand the awfulness of sin. Remember, don't blame God for sickness and death—blame sin. It is *our* sin—not just Adam's sin. The Bible tells us in Romans 5 that because we are children of Adam, we are just as much to blame as Adam.

L is for **Lord**, who reigns up on high,
The One who told Adam, "Obey, or you'll die."
Adam and Eve couldn't hide from their sin,
"Out of my garden, and don't come back in!"

These notes also apply for "N."

Why did God send Adam and Eve out of the garden? One of the main reasons is given in Genesis 3:22–24:

"And the Lord God said, Behold, the man is become as one of us, to know good and evil: and now, lest he put forth his hand and take also of the tree of life, and eat, and live forever: Therefore the Lord God sent him forth from the garden of Eden, to till the ground from whence he was taken. So he drove out the man. . . . "

Because God was going to provide a way for all humans to have the opportunity to come back to live with Him forever, He had to chase Adam away from the garden and not let him have access to the tree of Life.

God had to bring in the judgment of death so Jesus could come and die for sin.

Notice in Genesis 3:8–10, we are told that Adam and Eve tried to hide from God. Imagine, until they sinned, they loved to be in God's presence! God must have told Adam many wonderful things about how He had made the world. Imagine talking with our Creator and hearing Him talk back! That would really be something.

But sin spoiled all of this. We are now separated from God.

We all have heard of someone who has died. When a special friend or close relation dies, we feel sad because we are now separated from that person. He has left his body, and we will not be able to talk with him until we get to heaven providing we are going there.

If the separation we feel between us and a loved one is so great and so sad, how much greater and sadder must the separation be between us and God. But it is not God who has gone away from us. We have gone away from God because of our sin—our rebellion.

So often we do things throughout the day without even thinking about God—and yet the Bible says that He is thinking about us all the time. Again, we need to be reminded that the separation we feel is not God's fault—it is **our** fault!

A point of interest here concerns the location of the Garden of Eden. In Genesis 2:10 we are told: "And a river went out of Eden to water the garden: and from thence it was parted, and became into four heads." In Genesis 2:11–14 we are told the names of these rivers. Many Christians think that the Garden of Eden was located where the present Tigris and Euphrates Rivers are in the Middle East. However, these rivers today do **not** fit the description of the one source breaking into four rivers as described in Genesis. Not only this, but the Tigris and Euphrates Rivers are currently located on top of thousands of feet of layers that were laid down by the Flood.

As we will learn later, the global Flood totally destroyed the earth, and therefore would have destroyed the Garden of Eden. Noah would have used some of the names of rivers and areas that were familiar to him from before the Flood to name the new rivers and areas after the Flood. This is just as we have seen when people from England took similar names to Australia.

When Christians tell their children that the Garden of Eden was located in the Middle East where the present Tigris and Euphrates Rivers are today, they have erroneously taught them two things:

1. Noah's Flood was not a global event destroying the earth.

2. You don't have to take the words of the Bible seriously, since the description of the Garden of Eden does **not** fit the description of this area today.

It is so important to build our thinking on the Bible, and not on other people's opinions.

Student Exercise

Look at an Atlas of the Middle East where the Tigris and Euphrates Rivers are located. Trace the rivers onto a piece of paper.

Look up the description of the Garden of Eden in Genesis 2:10–14, and draw out the rivers as described. Compare the two.

Do you think the Tigris and Euphrates Rivers are today the same ones mentioned in Genesis 2? Why not?

M is for **Moan**, what a mess sin did make.
Thorns, thistles and death, and cursed ground for man's sake.
God had to judge sin, He's so holy and pure,
But God is so good, He provided a cure.

Genesis 3:17–18 states:

"And unto Adam he said, Because thou hast hearkened unto the voice of thy wife, and hast eaten of the tree, of which I commanded thee, saying, Thou shalt not eat of it: cursed is the ground for thy sake; in sorrow shalt thou eat of it all the days of thy life; Thorns also and thistles shall it bring forth to thee; and thou shalt eat the herb of the field."

The Dodo bird summarizes this nicely: "Things are getting worse!"

Again, the children need to understand that big changes occurred in this once-perfect world. From now on, the ground would not be as good as it was originally. It would be harder to get plants to grow. Now thorns and thistles would start to grow. God may have changed some of the plants so they would not be very nice. They would have thorns and cause lots of work for Adam to clear them away.

We all know that if we do not take special care of our gardens and lawns, they will soon be full of weeds. In fact, we pay a lot of money for poisons to try to stop the weeds ("thorns and thistles") from growing. Ask any farmer how hard it is to grow crops, and he will tell you that he spends a lot of time and money trying to keep the weeds out. God has certainly cursed the ground—and it really does cause us lots of "sorrow."

Now you know why it is that "thorns and thistles" will grow much more easily than our nice flowers or vegetables.

Every time we weed the garden, spray poisons for weeds, or watch a farmer getting weeds out of his field, we should be reminded of the curse that was placed on the world because of our sin. This is a continual reminder that we are sinful people. We live in rebellion against God and need to repent of our sin.

Therefore, thorns and thistles (weeds) should remind us of the following:

a. There was once a perfect world without thorns and thistles.

b. The first man Adam sinned, and sin spoiled the perfect world.

c. God had to judge sin. As part of that judgment, He cursed the ground and caused thorns and thistles to grow. He made it harder for humans to grow plants in the ground.

d. Thorns and thistles (weeds) should remind us of our sin and God's judgment.

e. One day in the future there will be a new earth and the curse will be removed (Revelation 22:3). There will be *no* thorns and thistles in the new earth!

Something else that is very interesting to consider concerns what happened when Jesus was arrested and crucified. When Jesus died on the cross, He took our sin and paid the penalty of death so we can be redeemed (brought back to God—thus mending the broken relationship).

Because of sin, death entered the world and God cursed the earth and brought forth thorns and thistles.

Consider:

a. Adam ate from the "tree of death," which is why death came into the world. When Jesus was crucified, He died on a tree (the cross). The wood of which the cross was made came from a tree that was a descendant of one of the trees God had made in the perfect world. Jesus suffered the very same curse of death He placed upon the world so we could live with Him forever.

b. Matthew 27:29 states: "And when they had plaited a crown of thorns, they put it upon his head, and a reed in his right hand: and they bowed the knee before him, and mocked him, saying, Hail, King of the Jews!"

Thorns were a result of the curse. When they crucified our Lord, they put thorns on His head—big thorns that dug into His scalp and hurt more than we can imagine. The thorn Adam has in his foot in the illustration is nothing compared to what happened to Jesus. He allowed Himself to suffer the horrible effects of the curse—the terrible thorns, as He died for our sins. Really, He has not asked us to suffer anything less than He suffered Himself. How great is our God!

Student Exercise

Bible research project: Read Genesis 3:14–24 carefully. Make a list of all the changes listed here because of sin. (See if you can get more than 18!)

N is for **Never**, no more could they go,
Back to the garden, where rivers did flow.
Angels with sword now stood at the gate,
What was in store, and what was their fate?

See notes for "L."

Genesis 3:22–24 states: "And the Lord God said, Behold, the man is become as one of us, to know good and evil: and now, lest he put forth his hand, and take also of the tree of life, and eat, and live forever: Therefore the Lord God sent him forth from the garden of Eden, to till the ground from whence he was taken. So he drove out the man; and he placed at the east of the Garden of Eden cherubims, and a flaming sword which turned every way, to keep the way of the tree of life."

In "L," we learned that God sent Adam and Eve out of the garden so they could not eat of the tree of life and thus live forever in their sinful rebellious state.

To make sure that Adam and Eve could not return to the garden, God put angels with a flaming sword to guard the entrance.

Ask the children why there would not be a place on earth today where angels with flaming swords would be guarding the entrance to the garden (remind them what was said in the notes for "L").

Share with the children that in Revelation 22:14, certain people (those who love the Lord) will gain access to the tree of life. As we go through this study, we will learn more about how to make sure a person will be able to "have a right to the tree of life."

Note that the Dodo bird makes the statement, "There's no going back." Adam and Eve could not go back to the tree of life in the garden. As we will find out, they had to look forward to the tree of life in the New Earth—but lots of very special and interesting events had to happen before this could occur.

Student Exercise

Use a concordance or Bible dictionary to help the children look up the words "Cherubims" and "Cherub." Try to make a detailed description of what Cherubims looked like and what special things they did.

O is for **Offering**, an animal was killed.
Because of their sin, blood had to be spilled.
But over and over this had to be done,
Till Christ on the cross the victory had won.

P is for **Plan**, which God always had,
Because he knew man, would turn very bad.
A few thousand years later, God's Son came to be,
A wonderful Savior for you and for me.

Genesis 3:21 states: "Unto Adam also and to his wife did the Lord God make coats of skins, and clothed them."

God now made clothes for Adam and Eve—clothes of animal skins. This means at least one animal had to be killed so its skin could be used.

This is the first time an animal died. Obviously, for an animal to be killed and skinned, blood would be shed. God sacrificed an animal because of Adam's sin.

This ties in beautifully with Hebrews 9:22, ". . . and without shedding of blood is no remission." For the remission of sin, blood has to be shed. By the way, this also means that there could not have been the shedding of blood millions of years before the first man sinned—this would undermine the meaning of bloodshed in relation to sin. The whole meaning of atonement would be destroyed.

We read in Leviticus 17:11 that "The life of the flesh is in the blood: and I have given it to you upon the altar to make an atonement for your souls: for it is the blood that maketh an atonement for the soul."

We can assume that God explained to Adam and Eve the significance of this event. He would have told them that because of sin, an offering had to be made to atone for sin. Because death was a consequence of sin and the "life of the flesh is in the blood," then blood had to be shed. They were no doubt instructed to sacrifice an animal as a sign that they acknowledged their sin and needed forgiveness.

This also helps us understand why in Genesis 4:5 God rejected Cain's offering. Genesis 4:3 tells us that Cain brought an offering of the "fruit of the ground"— *not* a blood sacrifice. Abel brought an animal as a sacrifice. Cain should have traded some of his "fruit of the ground" with Abel for an animal sacrifice—but he did not want to do it God's way.

This is also a good example to remind the children that it is very important to do things God's way. You can even be diligent in wanting to serve God—Cain wanted to bring a sacrifice—but if you don't serve God the way He instructs you, then He will not accept what you are doing.

Adam and Eve would have explained to their children every thing God had told them to do because of sin.

Notice that the dead animal in the illustration for "O" is a lamb. John 1:29 and 36 tells us that Jesus is "the lamb of God."

The Israelites had to sacrifice a lamb because of sin. The first mention of a lamb for sacrifice is in Genesis 22:7, "And Isaac spake unto Abraham his father, and said, My father: and he said, Here am I, my son. And he said, Behold the fire and the wood: but where is the lamb for a burnt offering?"

In Exodus chapter 12 the passover was instituted and the Israelites were to sacrifice a lamb. This, of course, was looking forward to the "lamb" that would be sacrificed "once for all" (Hebrews 10:10).

The point is that no matter how many animals were sacrificed for sin—their blood would never ultimately take away our sin. As it is stated in Hebrews 10:4, "For it is not possible that the blood of bulls and of goats should take away sins." There needed to be a sacrifice that would "once for all" cleanse away our sin. But this sacrifice would have to be a perfect man—another Adam.

In Exodus 12:5, the Israelites are told "Your lamb shall be without blemish. . . ."

Compare this to 1 Peter 1:19 which refers to Jesus: "But with the precious blood of Christ, as of a lamb without blemish and without spot." Christ was provided as another Adam—a perfect man (a perfect lamb) to shed His blood for sin.

Genesis does not tell us that the animal God killed to make skins was a lamb, but, on the basis of the rest of Scripture, we believe it is a valid assumption.

Notice in the illustration that Adam and Eve are dressed in lambs skins! Here we also have the origin of clothing. Think about it—a blood sacrifice as a covering for their sin—what a beautiful picture of what was to come in Christ.

It is important for the children to understand that the covering Adam and Eve made for themselves was good enough to cover their nakedness, but not their sin. Man cannot by himself cover his sin. God is the only one who can. God did this for Adam and Eve—He provided the lamb and the covering.

When God sent Jesus to die for our sins, He provided the lamb and the covering for our sin. This is a gift from God. A free gift if we will accept it (Romans 5:16–18).

The fact that God gave clothes because of sin also means that there is a moral basis for clothing. Because sin distorts everything, sin also distorts nakedness. Thus, we must construct a standard of clothing in accord with the reason clothing was given in the first place.

Imagine the horror on Adam and Eve's faces when for the first time they saw an animal die. Look at the illustration for "O." The look on the Dodo bird and Adam and Eve tell it all.

Be sure to again emphasize that those people who say the world could be millions of years old, and thus the fossil record (a record of billions of dead things—some with diseases, evidence of suffering, cruelty and lots of bloodshed) is millions of years old, undermine totally this vital and special message concerning the shed blood for sin.

There can be *no* shedding of blood before sin. Otherwise, the foundation of the Gospel message is destroyed. The meaning of every thing is tied up with its origin, and the meaning of death and bloodshed is dependent on its origin as described in Genesis.

Note: You will notice that Adam and Eve still have their fig leaf clothing on for L, M, and N. Because the section dealing with the blood sacrifice did not come until "O," we left them in their fig leaves until the shedding of blood was explained in "O." When you read Genesis Chapter 3, although you cannot dogmatically assert this, it is probable that the killing of the lamb occurred in the garden. However, we thought it was more important that Adam and Eve not be dressed in lamb's skin until the picture in "O" explained what had happened. If you like, when you get to "O," you can explain to the children that the killing of the lamb probably happened in the garden before they were actually thrown out.

Student Exercise

Read the following and try to answer the questions:

Imagine you are walking along a path in the woods when you come across a dead rabbit that has obviously been dead for a few days. At the same time you see a small dead tree beside the path.

Would you pick up the dead rabbit?

Would it worry you to pick up the dead tree (assuming it is very small)?

Why do you think you feel the way you do about a dead rabbit? (**Hint:** Plants were given for food. Animal death is an intrusion).

P is for **Plan**, which God always had,
Because he knew man, would turn very bad.
A few thousand years later, God's Son came to be,
A wonderful Savior for you and for me.

Q is for **Quiet**, Adam and Eve must have been,
When God spoke the words, of Genesis three verse fifteen.
God's Son came to die and be raised from the dead,
So to Hell we'd not go, but to Heaven instead.

Please make sure you also refer to the notes for "O."

We have discussed earlier that the plan of salvation was worked out from the foundation of the world. (Revelation 13:8).

In the illustration for "P," Adam is holding a scroll that pictures the major events of history leading up to the cross: Creation—Fall—Curse—Flood.

We don't know how much God told Adam, but at the same time He sacrificed the first animal, He no doubt told Adam and Eve that there was a plan already worked out. Adam and Eve probably did not understand all the details, but they knew that God was going to provide a way for them to be restored to their previous situation before sin.

In the illustration for "Q," we see the rest of the major events of history: Resurrection—Judgment by fire—New heaven and Earth—Hell.

It is important for children to know that even though there is a plan of salvation, there is also eternal judgment for those who do not trust in the Lord. The Dodo bird says it all when, pointing to the picture of Hell, he states: "Boys and girls, make sure you don't go there."

It would be great at this stage to make the children aware of Hell. Tell them that they *can* make sure they are not going there by trusting in the Lord Jesus who died for their sins. Maybe they might want to pray right after they read this. Help them to understand that they can *know* they are going to Heaven (John 3:16; Romans 10:9; Ephesians 1:13).

Genesis 3:15 states: "And I will put enmity between thee and the woman, and between thy seed and her seed: it shall bruise thy head, and thou shalt bruise his heel."

This is called the "proto-Gospel." In other words, we know that this is a reference to the death and resurrection of Christ. How much of this Adam and Eve understood, we do not know.

Some have suggested that when Eve had given birth to Cain and said ". . . I have gotten a man from the Lord" (Genesis 4:1), she thought somehow that he would be the man that would save them. However, if she did think this, her thoughts would have been shattered when Cain killed Abel.

Show the children that Genesis 3:15 really is a reference to Jesus dying on the cross. In fact, there are many references throughout the Old Testament that prophesy the events of the birth, death and resurrection of Christ (e.g., Psalm 22).

R is for **Rough**, how life had become,
The effects of God's curse had really begun.
Adam worked hard to obtain food to eat,
He made lots of sweat, so he must have been beat!

Genesis 3:19 states: "In the sweat of thy face shalt thou eat bread, till thou return unto the ground; for out of it wast thou taken: for dust thou art, and unto dust shalt thou return."

Adam was told he would have to work very hard to get food. In the garden, God had provided food for Adam while he looked after the plants; now, sin had changed things and obtaining food would be hard work.

It is hard work to produce food. Farmers have to plow the ground, fertilize it, water it, keep the pests away, keep the weeds out, harvest, and process it.

Take particular note that on the scroll in the illustration for "P," the cross is the final picture. In the illustration for "Q," the cross is the first picture. The cross is central to the Christian message.

Romans 5:9 tells us that we are justified by the blood of Jesus. The fact that the Father raised Jesus from the dead is *proof* that the Father accepted what His son did for us. This is the reason Paul tells us in 1 Corinthians 15:17: "And if Christ be not raised, your faith is vain; ye are yet in your sins." The cross is central to the Gospel—it is the power of the Gospel.

The last picture before hell in the illustration for "Q," is of the New Heaven and New Earth. Because sin ruined the present earth, 2 Peter 3:10 tells us this present earth is to be "burned up." Then in 2 Peter 3:13, we are told there will be a "New Heavens and a New Earth, wherein dwelleth righteousness." In other words, a place where there will be no sin and no curse. We also read about this in Revelation 21:1.

Student Exercise

Read Isaiah 7; Isaiah 53; Micah 5; Psalm 22.

What events do you recognize in these passages that refer to Jesus hundreds of years before they happened?

List as many as you can.

The world was no longer a perfect place. God was no longer sustaining the world perfectly, and things had started to run down.

The Dodo bird is making a very important statement: "I hope I don't become extinct." Of course, we know that today Dodo birds are (presumably) extinct. The point is that because of sin, the whole of creation was affected.

Romans 8:20–22: "For the creature was made subject to vanity, not willingly, but by reason of him who hath subjected the same in hope. Because the creature itself also shall be delivered from the bondage of corruption into the glorious liberty of the children of God. For we know that the whole creation groaneth and travaileth in pain together until now."

The Dodo bird's statement is a hint that sin is going to affect it also. Later, we see that the Dodo bird disappears from the page as it becomes extinct—but then it returns with a twinkle in its eye in "Z!"

Adam does not look like a primitive. He has made a tool that looks similar to something we would make today. After all, we have already stated that Adam was highly intelligent. Make sure you point this out to the children.

Here is another example of a doctrine based upon Genesis. The doctrine of work. Even before sin, Adam had to work to look after the garden; but after sin, the work would be hard, and not necessarily enjoyed. Remember, Paul wrote in 2 Thessalonians 3:10, "For even when we were with you, this we commanded you, that if any would not work, neither should he eat."

There are many people today who don't want to work. They just want everything handed to them. We should not be like this. We should want to work because God told us to. Certainly there are people who have problems finding a job to earn money today, and we should try to help them. However, they need to work hard, regardless. There are always plenty of things to do and people to help.

Student Exercise

a. Conduct a research project on the Dodo bird. Find out all you can about this bird and what the scientists think happened to it. This will help you identify more with our little character in the illustrations.

b. None of us like to do chores around the house. Why don't you ask your parents for a list of chores (if you don't have them already) that you can do each day/week. Next, make a real effort to ensure these are completed. Remind yourself that because of sin, work will be hard—but it must be done. This will be great training for you for the future.

S is for **Seventy**, and maybe lots more,
Imagine their family with children galore.
Long before Moses, when people were few,
Brothers and sisters could marry, that's true!

Genesis 5:4, in summing up the children Adam had during his lifetime, makes this statement: ". . . and he begat sons and daughters."

The famous Jewish historian, Josephus, records that according to Jewish tradition, Adam and Eve had 33 sons and 23 daughters. The Bible doesn't tell us the exact number, it just says they had "sons and daughters." Since Adam lived for 930 years (Genesis 5:5), there was plenty of time to have lots of children.

The most asked question concerning Genesis is probably the following: "Where did Cain find his wife?"

Some people believe there had to be other people created in addition to Adam and Eve so Cain could have a wife. However, we have already shown in the notes for "D" that this cannot be so.

Now consider the following:

1 Corinthians 15:45 tells us that Adam was the "first man."

Genesis 3:20 states that Eve was "the mother of all living."

Acts 17:26 tells us that all people are of "one blood," and therefore *all* people are related.

Thus, if there was only *one* man and *one* woman and *all* people are related in the first generation, brothers had to marry sisters.

There was no problem with this *originally*, because the law that close relations could no longer marry did not come into being until the time of Moses. We read about this in Leviticus 18. As long as marriage was one man for one woman for life, as discussed earlier, there was no problem with a brother and sister marrying—originally.

Actually, when you think about it—you *do* marry your relation. This is the reason Adam and Eve were the grandparents of us all. If they were not, then the whole Gospel message becomes meaningless. Why?

Paul tells us in 1 Corinthians 15:45 that Jesus is called the "last Adam." You see, the first Adam brought death into the world. He was the representative head of the entire human race. Thus all his descendants would suffer the problem of sin and death. We sin in Adam. We die in Adam.

Therefore, there was needed a new Adam to be a *new* representative head. But he would have to be a perfect man—and it would have to be someone of the same blood (that is—related to all people). This person would have to pay the penalty for sin, which is death. He would have to shed blood and show that this was acceptable to God. He would have to be raised from the dead, thus conquering death. But, he could not be any one of us since we are all sinners. God's solution was to provide another Adam. Jesus Christ, the Creator and the Son of God, became a man—a descendant of Adam (born of a virgin), but 100 percent God. He had two natures—God and man, but He was one person.

Our Creator became our relative, so He could die for all his relations—all people. This is why Paul states: "For as in Adam all die, even so in Christ shall all be made alive" (1 Corinthians 15:22).

What a message!

Now, back to Cain's wife. Some people say, "If you marry your relation, won't there be deformities in the children?" This is likely to happen in today's world if you marry your *close* relation.

We all have mistakes in our genes because of the curse. These mistakes add up year after year. Actually, the whole human race (like all living creatures) is running down—the opposite of what should be happening if evolution were true.

Before sin, there were no mistakes in Adam and Eve's genes. However, as a result of the curse, mistakes started to occur. These have accumulated over the years. Thus, the farther back in history you go the fewer mistakes, until before sin there were zero mistakes.

If close relations married today, they would be more likely to have similar mistakes in their genes. These mistakes can then combine and cause problems in the offspring. The farther away in relationship you are, the more likely it is that you will have different mistakes. If you married, the good genes from one partner tend to override the bad ones from the other. (See *The Answers Book,* page 177.)

Remember, Abraham was married to his half sister.

It is vital that we understand that *all* humans are related—and we are *all* now related to Jesus Christ because He became a man.

1 Corinthians 15:20 sums it up nicely: "But now is Christ risen from the dead, and become the firstfruits of them that slept." This means that because He rose, we will be raised!

Student Exercise

Have the children draw up a family tree beginning with Adam and continuing to Noah. After this, they can research their family tree as far back as Mom and Dad can help them. Have other parts of the family tree coming from Noah and going to famous people (e.g., the leaders of their country, etc.). Also have one line leading to Jesus—emphasizing that Jesus is related to everyone, and that is why He could die for all.

T is for **Trouble**, OH!, such a sad day,
Cain struck brother Abel, and dead there he lay.
The Lord punished Cain for what he had done,
But things still got worse, there was much more to come.

We have already discussed the problem with Cain's offering in "O."

Cain did not like God rejecting his offering. He was so angry that he killed his brother Abel. This was the world's first murder.

In Genesis 9:6, after the Flood, God brought in the death penalty for anyone who was a murderer. God certainly punished Cain. He put some sort of mark on Cain as a warning to others (Genesis 4:15). God also told Cain that the earth would not produce for him as it would for others. There was an extra special curse on the ground associated with Cain.

After Cain killed Abel, the Bible tells us that Cain went to the land of Nod (or "wandering") (Genesis 4:16). Some people read the Bible incorrectly here and think it says Cain found his wife in the land of Nod. However, he could easily have been married *before* he went to the land of Nod. The Bible tells us that Cain *"knew"* (had sexual relations with) his wife when he was in the land of Nod.

One of the things to point out to children is that sin is such a terrible thing that in just one generation after Adam and Eve, a person became a murderer. There have now been about six thousand years of sin with the curse operating on this earth. Sin is a terrible "disease."

Student Exercise

The Dodo bird in the illustration is dressed like a reporter. His notes say "World's first murder."

Have the children pretend they are the Dodo bird writing a report on this event. What happened? Why? What were the consequences? If you were able to take a photograph, what would be the best picture to illustrate what happened?

Question: What do you think happened to Abel after he died?

U is for **Utterly** shocking and bad.

People were killing, it became quite a fad!
God said, "That's enough! The world I will judge."
He sent a great flood—which made lots of sludge.

The feet of humans and animals sticking out of the mud while the Ark floats on top of the water is a graphic picture representing what happened during this great catastrophic event.

The Dodo bird, of course, is safe in the Ark!

Since there was no death of animals or man before sin, then how does one explain billions of dead things buried in rock layers, laid down by water all over the earth? To form fossils, an animal or plant would have to be buried quickly so it would not rot.

The Flood of Noah's day provides just these conditions. Lots of water (from above and below—Genesis 7:11) which would have caused massive erosion and sedimentation. All the right conditions to form billions of dead things, buried in rock layers, laid down by water all over the earth!

Some people today try to say that this Flood was only a local event. However, consider the following:

a. God put a rainbow in the sky **after** the Flood as a sign He would never send such a Flood again (Genesis 9:13–17). There have been **lots** of floods since, but they have all been local. God did not break His promise because we have **not** seen a **global** flood since Noah's time.

b. The event of Noah's Flood is used as a warning that there will be future judgment by fire (Matthew 24; 2 Peter 3, etc.). The future judgment will be a **global** judgment—just like the past judgment.

c. The language of Genesis 6–9 overwhelmingly speaks of a global catastrophe.

According to the Bible's chronology, the Flood of Noah's day was approximately 4500 years ago. This means most of the fossils in the earth are around 4500 years or younger. Presumably there would have been little fossilization from the Fall to the Flood since the climate would have been fairly stable. Since the Flood, there have been many local catastrophes and

some fossils would have formed *after* the Flood. Most of the fossil record would be the graveyard of the Flood.

Student Exercise

Read through Genesis chapters 6 through 9. List any words that speak of the global nature of this Flood. (e.g., whole, highest, etc.). Even if the same word is used more than once, list it each time it is used.

After doing this, ask yourself this question: Does the language of Genesis 6–9 speak of the Flood as just a local event or global one?

V is for **Violent**, were the waters of the flood,
People and animals were buried in the mud.
But God saved Noah, wife, daughters and sons,
Along with the animals in an ark weighing tons.

Look carefully at the sign on the Ark. "Lots and lots and lots and lots (including dinosaurs) and lots of animals on board."

We have already discussed earlier that there are far fewer created *kinds* of animals than there are varieties. Thus, when God sent two of each of the unclean and 7 of the clean animals on board the Ark, there were not as many animals as people think. In their famous book, *The Genesis Flood*, Dr. Morris and Dr. Whitcomb state: "There was need for no more than 35,000 individual vertebrate animals on the Ark." And there was plenty of room.

Genesis 7:7 tells us that only eight people went into the Ark. I am sure that in the last seven days while the Ark was being loaded and the door was still opened, Noah was warning people, "Come into the Ark and be saved—the judgment by water is coming." Sadly, only his sons and their wives went on board with him.

In a similar way today, we should be preaching a message like this: "Come to the Lord Jesus and be saved—the judgment by fire is coming."

Point out to the children that even though people today might say that the majority of scientists don't believe the Bible and don't believe in past or future judgment, the majority in Noah's day did not believe it either. What happened to the majority of people in Noah's day? They drowned! Just because the majority believe (or don't believe) something does not mean they are right! The Bible tells us that "Wide is the gate, and broad is the way, that leadeth to destruction, and many there be which go in thereat" (Matthew 7:13). John 3:19 states: that "men loved darkness rather than light. . . ."

Just as Noah and his family made sure they were safe in the Ark, each one of us need to make sure we are safe in Jesus, and that we have trusted in Him to save us from the future judgment.

The beginning of Chapter 8 in Genesis is a wonderful statement: "And God remembered Noah. . . ." When you think of how violent the flood waters must have been, how could Noah, his family and the animals survive? Well God tells us that He specially looked after Noah. Noah, his family and the animals were not out of God's thoughts for one moment.

You know, just as God "remembered Noah" in the midst of such a horrible catastrophe, He remembers each one of us moment by moment. Isn't that a comforting thought!

By the way, note that dinosaurs *were* on board the Ark!

Student Exercise

Get a number of families to go to a park or some large area. Measure the approximate size of Noah's Ark and have people stand at the corners and along the way. You could use colored string to mark it out. Take some pictures for your scrap book.

The Ark's measurements were:

Length: 437 feet/133.2 meters

Breadth: 73 feet/22.2 meters

Height: 44 feet/13.4 meters (You won't be able to picture this—but it would be something like the height of a 4 story building).

Let's hope that people come along and ask what you are doing. Have some tracts ready to hand out to them—perhaps our dinosaur booklet, *Dinosaurs and the Bible*. This could be a special day for witnessing.

W is for **Walk**; they came out of the ark.

The world was so different, the Flood left its mark.
Had people now learnt God's Word to obey?
They certainly did not, it is so sad to say.

Noah, his family and the animals (including dinosaurs) came out of the Ark. Notice the Dodo bird is still with us.

What was the first thing Noah did? He sacrificed one of every clean animal (Genesis 8:20). This would have been one of the greatest sacrifices ever! Noah was thankful to God for saving him. He recognized that God was just in sending the Flood because He is a righteous judge.

Noah also knew that the judgment came because of sin and that blood had to be shed for sin. Even though Noah was saved on the Ark, he recognized that he was still a sinner and had to make sacrifices for sin.

The Ark is a beautiful picture of Jesus Christ. Noah had to go through a door to be saved, and so must we go through a door (Jesus—John 10:9) to be saved. The Ark saved Noah from the judgment and Jesus will save us from the fiery judgment of Hell.

The Ark landed in the area we now know as the Middle East. Therefore, this means that *every* type of land animal (including kangaroos, elephants, dinosaurs, etc.) once lived in the Middle East. These animals would have started to breed and move around the earth. After the Flood there would have been much evaporation because the oceans were warmer (remember, most of the water came from under the ground). This would have produced great storms with snow and ice and ultimately caused an Ice Age.

As water left the oceans and was turned into snow and ice, the ocean levels would have dropped, forming land bridges around the world. The animals would move to other continents over these land bridges.

Also, ever since the time of Noah people have built boats and sailed around the world, often taking their favorite animals with them. Thus, animals would have spread around the world. Each kind would end up forming different varieties within a kind as they separated and went in other directions. This explains why you have different varieties of bears, elephants, horses, and so on.

Wouldn't you think that this Flood would have left such an impression around the world and in the minds of the people on board, that as the population grew after the Flood they would not disobey God? Due to their sinful nature, the people very quickly forgot the judgment of God. As we will see next, they rebelled against God again.

Student Exercise

Draw a picture of an animal fossil (or copy one out of a book). As you look at it, write down all the things you are reminded of concerning the past and the future. You should be able to get a long list. Think about the great sermon you could preach using a fossil and God's Word.

(**Hint:** Death after sin: no death in future; past judgment; no evolution).

X is in **eXplode**, the population sure grew,
But what happened next, read God's Word for the clue.
They built a great tower to reach to the sky,
For God's spoken Word, they were quick to defy.

Y is for **Yes**, God did soon judge their sin,
By confusing their language—what a terrible din!
He scattered the people all over the place,
Till God's final judgment, we'll all have to face.

Genesis 9:1 states: "And God blessed Noah and his sons, and said unto them, Be fruitful and multiply, and replenish the earth."

God commanded the people to spread out over the earth and fill it. However, we find in Genesis 11 that the people who spoke the one language defied God by staying together and building a tower. This structure was probably a worship center associated with an evil religion which worshipped the moon and the stars instead of God. Isn't it sad that people so quickly forget they are sinners and what God has done?

To make man spread out over the earth, God caused people to begin speaking in different languages, thus hindering their efforts to work together in rebellion against Him. Thus, they would not have been able to work together anymore. People would have split up and moved over the earth, and others would have gone and lived in caves until they were able to build houses.

Some people would have used stone tools until they found sources of metals and to make metal tools. However, others may have just kept on using the stone tools. Just because we find evidence that people used stone tools or lived in caves does not mean they were primitive. It would only indicate man's spreading out over the earth into new areas.

At this time, the human population would have dispersed causing the gene pool to break up. As groups of people went in different directions, they would have taken with them different combinations of information in their genes. Thus, the different types of people would have created tribes and nations and eventually resulted in Chinese, Japanese, Eskimo, etc. The characteristics such as skin color, eye shape and other features that distinguish the different groups are just minor differences. For instance, everyone has the same skin color. It is just a matter of how much or how little a person has of this color. The publication entitled, *"The Answers Book,"* has an excellent section explaining this in greater detail.

The Bible's record in Genesis is the only explanation for there being different language groups in the world.

Isn't it sad that because of man's sin, God had to give him different languages? This made it harder for people to work together in rebellion against God, but it also made it more difficult to proclaim to all the people the truth about God's Word. Praise the Lord that for years dedicated Christians have been translating God's Word into different languages so that all will be able to hear the wonderful truth about salvation.

In the illustration for "X," you will see that the Dodo bird is saying that he is going to become extinct. He is not in the next illustration. It wasn't the knock on the head that made him extinct, but due to sin and the harsh world after the Flood, lots of animals and plants completely vanished.

Everyone will be disappointed to see our little character leave, but he does appear again in "Z!"

Z is for **Zip**, so quick it will be,
When Jesus comes back for you and for me.
If our name is found in the "Lamb's Book of Life,"
We'll sure live forever in a place with no strife.

Read Revelation chapters 20–22. Take particular note of the following verses:

Revelation 20:12–15
Revelation 21:1–8
Revelation 21:27
Revelation 22:3
Revelation 22:12–14.

Explain to the children that all those who love the Lord Jesus and have asked Him into their hearts, believing and acknowledging that He is their Savior, will have their names written in the "Lamb's book of life."

However, the Bible clearly teaches that those who have not trusted the Lord Jesus will be judged and sent to a place of torment forever and ever! This should make every one of us want to ensure that we are saved, and tell everyone about this message.

This final section presents an opportunity to lead children to Christ if they have not made that commitment. It also is a great opportunity to pray for unsaved friends and loved ones.

Now that the children have all the background information, go through the plan of salvation from beginning to end using the information and Scriptures in the above notes. Use other Scriptures as well

Student Exercise

Have your parents take you to (or call) a local Bible Society. Find how many different languages there are in the world, and how many of these have had the Scriptures translated. Make a list of those languages which do not yet have God's Word translated. Why not make it a point each day to pray for the Lord to raise up people to translate His Word into these languages—maybe you will become a Bible translator someday!

(e.g., 1 John 1:9; Romans 3:23) to help them understand they need to repent of their sin.

This can be a special time to challenge each child to make a commitment to Christ. Write and tell us when commitments are made. We would love to hear from you! You may write to: Answers in Genesis, P.O. Box 6330, Florence, Kentucky, USA., 41022

Share Luke 15:10 with them: "Likewise, I say unto you, there is joy in the presence of the angels of God over one sinner that repenteth."

Student Exercise

Obtain a small book of blank pages and entitle it the "Lamb's Book of life." Write the names of people (including yourself, hopefully) who are Christians. On a separate sheet of paper, write the names of friends or relatives who are not Christians. Pray for them every day. When any of them become Christians, add their name to the book, and then show them what you did! You should also include names of our government leaders since God tells us to pray for them as well (1 Timothy 2:1–2).

A is for **Adam**; God made him from dust.
He wasn't a monkey, he looked just like us.
Although some scientists don't think it was so,
It was God who was there, and He ought to know.

B is for **Bible**, a book God did give,
To tell where we came from and how we should live.
We did not evolve, God made it so plain,
People are people, we stay just the same.

C is for **Creatures**; God made them all,
Some rather little, but others quite tall.
He said unto Adam, "What names do you think?"
Adam then named them, quick as a wink!

D is for **Dinosaur**, Dodo and Deer,
Like all of the animals, no man did they fear.
But even though all was in true harmony,
Adam then realized, "There's no one like me!"

E is for **Eve**, his beautiful bride,
God made just for Adam, from part of his side.
To sleep God did put him, and when he awoke,
"She's flesh of my flesh," were the words that he spoke.

F is for **Fruit**, God said not to take,
"Because if you do, much trouble you'll make!"
They lived in the garden God specially made,
And if they'd obeyed Him, they could have then stayed.

G is for **Ghastly**, is what happened next,
Let's go to the Bible, and look at the text.
In Genesis chapter three and verse one,
Eve met the serpent, but she didn't run.

H is for **How** very sly he did sound,
The Devil saw Eve and the fruit she had found.
"Did God really say, 'Don't eat from that tree?'
It'll open your eyes—you'll be wise, like me."

I is for **Interested**, Eve did become,
She picked off the fruit and then she ate some.
It tasted so nice, what harm could there be?
"Here Adam, eat some and come and join me."

J is for **Jovial**, as Satan must have been,
The Devil was gleeful with all he had seen.
He was able to trick poor Eve with a lie,
"Obey all my words, and you'll surely not die!"

K is for **Knew**; Adam saw he was bare.
Both he and his wife no clothes they did wear.
They sewed up some fig leaves, and then tried to hide,
As they suddenly realized the Devil had lied.

L is for **Lord**, who reigns up on high,
The One who told Adam, "Obey, or you'll die."
Adam and Eve couldn't hide from their sin,
"Out of my garden, and don't come back in!"

M is for **Moan**, what a mess sin did make.
Thorns, thistles and death, and cursed ground for man's sake.
God had to judge sin, He's so holy and pure,
But God is so good, He provided a cure.

N is for **Never**, no more could they go,
Back to the garden, where rivers did flow.
Angels with sword now stood at the gate,
What was in store, and what was their fate?

O is for **Offering**, an animal was killed.
Because of their sin, blood had to be spilled.
But over and over this had to be done,
Till Christ on the cross the victory had won.

P is for **Plan**, which God always had,
Because he knew man, would turn very bad.
A few thousand years later, God's Son came to be,
A wonderful Savior for you and for me.

Q is for **Quiet**, Adam and Eve must have been,
When God spoke the words, of Genesis three verse fifteen.
God's Son came to die and be raised from the dead,
So to Hell we'd not go, but to Heaven instead.

R is for **Rough**, how life had become,
The effects of God's curse had really begun.
Adam worked hard to obtain food to eat,
He made lots of sweat, so he must have been beat!

S is for **Seventy**, and maybe lots more,
Imagine their family with children galore.
Long before Moses, when people were few,
Brothers and sisters could marry, that's true!

T is for **Trouble**, OH!, such a sad day,
Cain struck brother Abel, and dead there he lay.
The Lord punished Cain for what he had done,
But things still got worse, there was much more to come.

U is for **Utterly** shocking and bad.
People were killing, it became quite a fad!
God said, "That's enough! The world I will judge."
He sent a great flood—which made lots of sludge.

V is for **Violent**, were the waters of the flood,
People and animals were buried in the mud.
But God saved Noah, wife, daughters and sons,
Along with the animals in an ark weighing tons.

W is for **Walk**; they came out of the ark.
The world was so different, the Flood left its mark.
Had people now learnt God's Word to obey?
They certainly did not, it is so sad to say.

X is in **eXplode**, the population sure grew,
But what happened next, read God's Word for the clue.
They built a great tower to reach to the sky,
For God's spoken Word, they were quick to defy.

Y is for **Yes**, God did soon judge their sin,
By confusing their language—what a terrible din!
He scattered the people all over the place,
Till God's final judgment, we'll all have to face.

Z is for **Zip**, so quick it will be,
When Jesus comes back for you and for me.
If our name is found in the "Lamb's Book of Life,"
We'll sure live forever in a place with no strife.

Recommended Creationist Resources:

Books

Adults:

The Genesis Record by Dr. Henry M Morris.
A verse by verse scientific and devotional commentary on Genesis. Very easy to read. A must for every home library.

The Lie: Evolution by Ken Ham.
A best seller that shows clearly why Christians cannot consistently believe in evolution and the Bible. Illustrates how *all* doctrines of theology have their foundation directly or indirectly in the book of Genesis. Shows the relationship between evolution and the ills of society such as abortion, homosexual behavior, suicide, lawlessness, etc.

The Answers Book by Ham, Snelling and Wieland.
A well illustrated book containing the most asked questions on Genesis and Creation/evolution answered in an easy-to-understand style. Answers to questions such as: Where did Cain get his wife? What is the origin of the races? Where did dinosaurs come from? What is carbon dating? And much more.

Creation: The Facts of Life by Dr. Gary Parker.
The classic arguments used for evolution as taught in colleges, public schools and the media, refuted by a Professor in Biology who taught these evidences before he became a Creationist.

The Amazing Story of Creation by Dr. Duane Gish.
The world's foremost Creationist debater presents the best scientific evidences for Creation and against evolution in this colorfully illustrated family book.

***Creation* Magazine**
Obtain a yearly subscription to this unique colorful and glossy family magazine that the whole family will enjoy. Contains Biblical and scientific articles that will help Christians to defend their faith and witness to others.

Children:

D is for Dinosaur by Ken and Mally Ham.
A colorful rhyme book for children, similar in style to *A is for Adam*, but concentrating particularly on dinosaurs.

Dinosaurs by Design by Duane Gish
Journey into the exciting world of dinosaurs. This book provides information that helps combat the evolutionary theories surrounding these incredible creatures.

The Great Dinosaur Mystery by Paul Taylor.
A beautifully illustrated book for the whole family that gives a Biblical perspective on dinosaurs.

Life Before Birth by Gary Parker.
A colorfully illustrated book to teach children about the development of a baby and instruct them against abortion.

Dry Bones and other Fossils by Gary and Mary Parker
The Parkers explain what fossils are and how they are formed. They demonstrate how fossils are evidence of Noah's Flood and not evolution.

Videos

Answers in Genesis seminar (12 tapes) with Ken Ham and Gary Parker
A complete Creation seminar, professionally videotaped and edited with audience reaction and large numbers of color illustrations. It covers the major Biblical and scientific topics associated with Creation/evolution and Genesis. Instructive, entertaining and suitable for age 10 and up, teenager and adult.

The Genesis Solution with Ken Ham
An acclaimed film with Ken Ham and illustrated with animation to help people understand the relevance of Creation. This is the message of the book, *The Lie: Evolution*, presented in a 45 minute sermon and professionally produced.

Children:

D is for Dinosaur (15 minutes)
The book *D is for Dinosaur* animated for children with an Australian girl narrating the rhymes. Quaint.

The Great Dinosaur Mystery (15 minutes)
Fascinating information about dinosaurs, showing evidence that they lived at the same time as man. Suitable for showing in public schools.

What Really Happened to the Dinosaurs with Ken Ham (45 minutes)
A fast moving presentation from the "Answers In Genesis" series that teaches children to understand dinosaurs from a Biblical perspective. Also teaches children how to think about the Creation/evolution issue.

To purchase or obtain further information on these resources, contact:

United States of America:

Answers in Genesis
P.O. Box 6330
Florence, Kentucky 41022 USA
Phone: 1-800-350-3232 or (606) 647-2900

Master Books
P. O. Box 26060
Colorado Springs, CO 80936 USA
Phone: 1-800-999-3777 or (719) 591-0800

Australia:

Creation Science Foundation
P.O. Box 6302
Acacia Ridge DC, QLD 4110, Australia
Phone: 617 3273-7650
Fax: 617 32737672

Canada:

Creation Science Association of Ontario
P.O. Box 831, Station A
Scarborough, Ontario, M1K 5C8, Canada

United Kingdom and Europe:

Creation Science Foundation (UK)
P.O. Box 1427
Sevenhampton, Swindon, Wilts.,
SN6 7UF, United Kingdom
Phone: (01793) 512268
Fax: (01793) 861462

New Zealand:

Creation Science Foundation (NZ)
215 Bleakhouse Road, Howick
Auckland
Phone: (09) 5348914
Fax: (09) 5374818